First, Heal Thyself

How to Survive Spiritually in the Healthcare Industry

Jamieson E. Jones, MD and
Nadine A. Kassity-Krich MBA, RN

iUniverse, Inc.
New York   Bloomington

First, Heal Thyself
How to Survive Spiritually in the Healthcare Industry

The information, ideas, and suggestions in this book are not intended as a substitute for professional medical advice. Before following any suggestions contained in this book, you should consult your personal physician. Neither the author nor the publisher shall be liable or responsible for any loss or damage allegedly arising as a consequence of your use or application of any information or suggestions in this book.

iUniverse books may be ordered through booksellers or by contacting:

iUniverse
1663 Liberty Drive
Bloomington, IN 47403
www.iuniverse.com
1-800-Authors (1-800-288-4677)

Because of the dynamic nature of the Internet, any Web addresses or links contained in this book may have changed since publication and may no longer be valid. The views expressed in this work are solely those of the author and do not necessarily reflect the views of the publisher, and the publisher hereby disclaims any responsibility for them.

ISBN: 978-1-4502-2220-4 (pbk)
ISBN: 978-1-4502-2218-1 (cloth)
ISBN: 978-1-4502-2219-8 (ebk)

Library of Congress Control Number: 2010905824

Printed in the United States of America

iUniverse rev. date: 6/10/2010

Dedication

This book is dedicated with overwhelming gratitude to the patients, co-workers, and mentors who have so generously nurtured our personal evolution. By planting the seeds of spiritual development you have touched us in ways that have enriched our careers and our lives.

J.J. and N.K.K.

Contents

Foreword

Jamieson E. Jones, MD and Nadine Kassity-Krich MBA RN began their respective careers the same year at San Diego Children's Hospital. Working together, they recognized a shared interest in the deeper meaning of life and of their profession. As healthcare professionals, they noticed how their profession tended to look outside of itself for the solution to discontent rather than looking within. They agreed the medical field was inclined to travel at the speed of light and tended to dismiss the calm, contemplative inner homework that is a necessary component of a true healer.

The deeper consciousness of healing seemed to have gotten lost in the increasingly business-oriented world of medicine. They observed similar feelings displayed by colleagues and began to think about how they could reinspire themselves and others to explore ways of reclaiming all that was originally in their hearts upon entrance into the profession. Over time, they developed an interest in integrating psychological and spiritual principles into their professional lives. This interest gradually turned into lectures and workshops, and soon colleagues were asking for these ideas to be put into a book.

This book is a response to those requests.

Preface

Put the field of medicine on the examination table and what do you find? You find a healthcare system that is sick. Put it on a psychiatrist's couch and you find a profession in the midst of a nervous breakdown.

It is an extraordinary time for healthcare—full of unusual possibilities and unforeseen pitfalls. Medicine's ever-increasing technologies are a blessing to the world, but these advances do not address the ever-increasing dissatisfaction and disconnect that both caregivers and patients are experiencing. The solution to these problems isn't going to be found simply in increased government funding or through better business models—we've tried those for decades. What is required is a different type of change—a more human prescription and a more deeply personal solution to the problems ailing medicine.

A recent visit to the cathedral of "St. John the Divine" near Columbia University in Manhattan revealed a barren cathedral, the altar and most of the interior removed for renovations. A cathedral without an altar appears an apt metaphor for the current state of medicine. Medicine seems as if it has been pulled from the more spiritual realm of the house-call doctor and bedside nurse and then pushed, initially, into the halls of science and then into an arena dominated by lawyers, businessmen, and insurance companies.

As healthcare workers, many of us feel akin to cathedrals without altars. We were highly trained and have earned revered initials after our names, but we lack a central core of meaning—an anchor of spirituality. We need and deserve a healthier balance between the spiritual and scientific aspects of our professions.

We are healers who are out of balance and separated from our spiritual core—our true, caregiving natures. We are wounded and in need of healing, in need of our own inner development. Many of us in the healing arts have a deeply spiritual nature, a nature that is buried by the complexities of our workplace. Those complexities block the ability to bring our deeper, spiritual uniqueness into the workplace. Yet we all know that spiritual nature exists—the same way we all know the seeds of spring exist even amid the harshest winter.

This inner development isn't something that you are going to find discussed in a standard exchange around a patient's bedside. In fact, it has become an almost furtive dialogue found in the far corners of hospitals and nursing homes. But truly conscious caregivers everywhere are seeking to increase their ability for compassionate connection with their patients and their co-workers and, thus, to reconnect with the deeper meaning and purpose in their jobs. This book is for them and for those who wish to join them.

We're All Caregivers

Healthcare professionals are the primary, but not the sole, targets of this book. In truth, becoming a caregiver is a role afforded to almost everyone at some point in their lives, although it often comes unexpectedly. We may find ourselves caring for aging parents, a sibling, a spouse, or maybe even a friend, without much forethought. A son or daughter may suddenly become the caregiver for a parent, or by dint of an ill spouse, a CEO may be cast in something other than his or her usual role. As our population ages, this broadening of lay caregiving is rapidly increasing.

The labyrinth of illness is not walked only by those who are ill, but by those, whether healthcare professionals or lay people, who accompany them on their journey. Thus, the discussions in this book offer insights into the world of conscious caregiving of whatever stripe. The groundwork for heightened spirituality exists underneath our feet, whether we walk the hallways of the hospital, visit our elders in a nursing home, or broach end-of-life discussions with a family member.

Bottom line—when we are suddenly thrust into the role of caregiver, we can make the experience more rewarding by deciding to adopt a more spiritual perspective.

Our Aim

This book aims to reinvigorate the heart of a languishing medical industry. That is a tall order, but a pernicious problem calls for a bold solution.

While medicine is ever-changing, this book seeks to reground you in what has not changed—the patient-caregiver encounter. We want to help you reclaim that relationship as central and sacred, to learn how to use the material of your day to renew your own personal meaning, and to put yourself back into the alchemy of healing. As we provide care to another we, in effect, enter their experience. In other words, the healer is not separate from the healing taking place.

As children, many of us probably heard from our parents the continual refrain, "Mind your own business." There is little in our culture that helps us to develop the caregiving part of our nature. Instead, we are more often encouraged to form a more self-centered focus, to watch out for ourselves, to compete and win.

But for many of us in the healing arts, our core, caregiving nature has persisted through all the cultural discouragements. That caregiving nature is our primary way of being. It is precultural, preverbal, and possibly even prenatal for most of us. We need to build the foundation of our career on the underpinnings of this caregiving nature, not on the changing tides of healthcare. How we work with this, apply this, and get this to grow requires a turning inward, a collaboration with our soul.

This book proposes solutions to the feeling of disconnection that permeates our professional lives. It explores our interrelationships with ourselves, our co-workers, our patients, and the system of healthcare as a whole. It seeks to infuse new understandings into that web of relationships and, by so doing, our professional connections and commitments have no other option than to become refreshed.

Filled with Opportunities

"Many are the uses of adversity," Shakespeare tells us. Instead of feeling like victims of a healthcare system that is rapidly changing in ways we do not like, maybe we should realize the opening this is giving us. Can we learn to see our daily work as filled with opportunities for personal growth? If so, some of our missing energy may be restored as new layers of meaning and richness in our jobs are revealed.

This is a chance to look past the obvious and uncover something much more profound, something more purposeful, and something that has been in healthcare all along but is often overlooked.

Adopting a Spiritual Perspective

Whether as a relative, friend, or professional, most enter a caregiving role with high ideals but soon confront a jarring reality posed by the day-to-day struggles of caring for another. The struggles are predictable and they probably will not change much, but what can change is the quality of presence of the caregiver. Expanding that quality of presence is the transformation sought by this book, a transformation that begins the progressive deepening of a caregiver's spiritual path.

Spirituality, for the purposes of this book, does not necessarily mean religion. It means connecting with others and ourselves at deeper and deeper levels.

In the discussions that follow, we take spiritual principles and practices from many religious traditions and apply them to situations encountered in one of the most stressful of life's circumstances, that of caregiver. Though the stakes may not be as dire for the nonprofessional as they are for professionals in a hospital setting, the dynamics of the caregiving interactions encompass similar issues. In both instances, integrating a spiritual perspective into caregiving helps us to become more conscious of our role. Thus, the context of caregiving is less relevant than the purpose and meaning that can be found in the task itself.

No Better Classroom

To heal ourselves and to heal healthcare, we must each do the personal work necessary to transform our everyday experience into something more heartfelt. Not everyone, of course, is interested in personal development. But for those who are, there is no better classroom, no better ashram or Zen center, than sitting with those that we care for when they are ill.

Too often we go to work and feel stymied by the business of healthcare rather than fulfilled by the spirituality of healing. We find no outlet for the nurturing nature that encouraged us to become doctors and nurses in the first place. But once we recognize that we do not need to settle for the strictly financial rewards our jobs offer, we are poised for change. We can then see that our deeper, personal need for meaning and purpose is a vital part of why we joined the healthcare profession.

As more and more of us find the inner core of spirituality in our workplace, we will begin to feel the full effect of our potential and that of our profession. The real unhealed healer is medicine itself.

We begin our journey by taking an in-depth look at the phenomenon of burnout—the pervasive symptom of disconnect that many feel in their roles. This book then performs a *diagnosis* by examining the evolution of the health sciences and the role of the caregiver. It then moves onto *treatment* by exploring psychological and spiritual techniques that can help mend both healer and patient. Finally, the *prognosis* in which we look at what an enlightened future can hold for the caregiver and for medicine

Acknowledgments

All books are a product of many influences. First and foremost, we would like to thank ourselves, or should we say each other. For any who write, you know the emotional commitment that it takes to manifest a book. Coauthoring has its own struggles, yet we have delighted in expanding our friendship through this material.

This book is a collage developed from the experiences, readings, inspirations, anecdotes, and contemplations of the authors in their interest to probe the rich spiritual potential in healthcare. By exploring the underdeveloped intersection between spiritual contemplation and clinical medicine, we add two more voices to the ongoing dialogue about the evolution of the healing arts.

We would also like to thank Kathy Hearn, who helped with ideas, Natasha Nikolai, who helped with organization, and Terrie Petrie and Dale Fetherling, who helped with writing and editing.

Both of us were fortunate to have fathers who were physicians back in a time that was untainted by our current business and malpractice paradigms. For their example of what medicine can be, for their love of their jobs and their patients, we gratefully acknowledge their influence in this book.

Nadine would like to thank her husband, David, for his unending support, and her mother, Barbara, who always knew this book would get published. Sophia and Gable, this book is written for you, the next generation, in hopes that an expanded sense of healing will nurture our collective evolutionary potential.

Part I: Diagnosis

Chapter 1
Burnout or Wake-Up?

"Something has to die in order for us to begin to know our truths."
—Adrienne Rich

Consider the evolution of one young healthcare worker's development. What does her experience tell you about how modern medicine colors the outlook of many of its practitioners?

> Asked why she wanted to become a physician, a first-year medical student told her class how her mother's struggle with lung cancer had inspired her. "When my mom got sick, I saw how much she suffered and how much she relied on the doctors and nurses to nurture her and make her better. For me, becoming a doctor was a way to pay tribute to all the people who devoted themselves to helping her."

> Five years later, near the end of her internship, the same young woman was asked a similar question, "What motivates you to come to work?" Without the slightest hesitation she replied, "Student loans."

> Within a year after finishing medical school, her dreams of healing had collapsed and money was the only tangible payoff she could see.

Many of us can relate to both her compelling, altruistic motivation and to her disillusion. That is in large part because there is no spiritual counterbalance to the exhausting demands of the medical routine. A more seasoned doctor expressed the same sentiments when he said, "I've traded lots of dreams for a bigger and bigger paycheck. Only recently have I realized what was happening."

In addition to feeling as if we've lost control of our professional lives, we forget that our profession is one of human engagement during some of life's most intense experiences. The economic logic that has been superimposed on healthcare is such a dominant focus that the deeper intentions of healthcare are lost or hidden. When we lose that connection to our profession, our patients often don't get what they need. As a veteran nurse stated, "I used to come to work excited to connect with my patients. Now, I am happy working nights because of the extra pay and also because most of my patients sleep through the night and require very little one-on-one time."

Why Medicine Attracts

When asked the classic "Why do you want to be in medicine?" question, most of us tried quite hard to avoid the stereotypical answer, "I want to help others." But as trite as the answer sounds, it was true for most of us. We were drawn into the healing arts, consciously or unconsciously, because of our caring and compassionate natures. In large measure, we're a group that seeks meaning in our life's work that is deeper than a mere paycheck.

Yet the demands of efficiency and documentation often come to supplant care of patients as the central focus of our workday. As a result, the spiritual rewards we receive in connecting with others are diminished and sometimes lost because we now spend so much time working on charts and other documentation. When we feel stymied by the business of healthcare rather than fulfilled by the spirituality of healing, we find no outlet for the nurturing nature that propelled us to become doctors and nurses in the first place.

Often, burnout is the rather predictable result of this role-based stagnation. Workshop titles at medical meetings often proclaim, "The Epidemic of Burnout" or "The Seven Habits to Avoid Burnout." By the time anything becomes a topic at seminars, it is usually commonplace.

In whatever area of medicine you work in, burnout is probably a standard complaint. Although it hardly seems necessary to describe burnout to contemporary healthcare workers, this chapter seeks to provide a new context in which to view the experience. We'll discuss burnout's significance in our careers as well as in our collective experience.

Symptoms Abound

We all recognize the symptoms of burnout—co-workers with gradually increasing sarcasm, the slow decline in the quality of their caring, and the increasingly frequent days when they come to work with vacant, uninterested eyes, perhaps even glancing at their watches with some frequency as you speak with them. Such signs of emptiness have become so prevalent that we can immediately diagnose the lack of vitality in our emotionally exhausted colleagues. In extreme cases, burned-out nurses and physicians leave medicine altogether in search of something more fulfilling.

Even more alarming is the day we look in the mirror and see our own hollow eyes staring back at us. At first we may dismiss this, knowing we work in a system that barely allows us to tread water. We may blame our symptoms on too many overtime shifts or too much night call, but we also may notice that we often feel too tired to give patients the attention they deserve. Usually that is when many of us slip totally into role-based behaviors and simply go through the motions at work. When this happens, we become disconnected not only from our patients and our co-workers, but also from *ourselves*. Ultimately, we end up feeling isolated and lonely, while our motivation, our inner life and ideals, seem lifeless. "Loneliness," Carl Jung said, "does not come from having no people about one, but from being unable to communicate the things that seem important to one's self."

A Wake-Up Call

Burnout is sometimes described as "the dark night of the soul." But in our case, it might be more accurately called "the dark night of our role." Burnout may feel like the end of a career, but if we dig deeper, we can see it is actually a place of a great potential. If we look more deeply, we see this crisis often comes to those who've dutifully followed a linear life plan, only to realize their soul yearns for more options.

Burnout is a big wake-up call, a time when the psyche screams for a change in consciousness. To really make burnout a growth experience requires no change in job content, but rather a change in context. Until we connect with this new context—that is, with the deeper, more authentic self that is trying to be heard—we'll continue the frustrating descent into this dark night. We've exchanged our creative selves for an approved role. In short, our souls have begun to starve.

But within every crisis lurks an opportunity. Just as a midlife crisis offers a chance to redefine self-worth and identity, burnout offers us a chance to let go of these limiting roles we've been trained to adopt. Burnout can magnify our clarity about the collapsed roles we've adopted and help catapult us in new directions.

The Role of Emotions

Healthcare workers, studies show, are highly prone to burnout. Researchers have found that "workers who have frequent intense or emotionally charged interactions with others are more susceptible to burnout" (Cordes and Doherty, 1993).[1] Though many are so burned out that they can't even feel that emotional charge, no amount of professional detachment can change the fact that suffering in others triggers our emotions.

As a doctor or a nurse, you're expected to care for the sick and the dying, but the collective code dictates that you must care for them without becoming emotionally involved. In the fast-paced world of healthcare, triggered feelings are often unexplored, and unexpressed emotions build up like debris behind a dam. This buildup is ignored at our own peril. Without supportive relationships with co-workers, administrators, or family members, it is hard to find an outlet for this often grueling emotional frustration.

When our emotions are not properly cared for or understood, a distance develops in the overextended practitioner. This protects us from the difficult parts of our job but, unfortunately, it also denies us the joy. When this happens, our enthusiasm diminishes, and we find our roles have cut us off from sharing our deepest gifts.

When in burnout mode, we feel something similar to post-call fatigue syndrome. We're so exhausted that we don't really care much about anything or anyone. There seems little point to anything we are doing. We start thinking that the patient's problems are trivial and silly, and before we realize it, we have replaced compassion with indifference.

We substitute listening to our patients with chatting with co-workers at the nurses' station or in the cafeteria. A voice inside us confusingly whispers, "Isn't it obvious to this patient that I'm the one who's exhausted and hurting?" Soon, the voice begins to scream, "What about me?" Then the downward cycle begins and we feel guilty for feeling this way. Post-call exhaustion is usually rectified with a good night's sleep. The exhaustion of burnout, on the other hand, isn't as responsive.

The combination of medicine and exhaustion are not new. For centuries, healthcare workers have been expected to log arduous hours. Some days, our profession forces us to use every ounce of energy and every piece of ourselves. Not surprisingly, after years of trying to maintain a balance between professionalism and compassion, our energy and emotions finally get tapped out.

This haunting feeling of emotional and physical depletion may not seem urgent, but if ignored long enough, it becomes a personal emergency. It can overtake our abilities to function fully. And if it isn't attended to, our

---

1   Academy of Management Review [AMR], 18, 621 - 659.

professional souls begin to gradually disintegrate. "Do no harm" is the first commandment in medical ethics, but this imperative is rarely, if ever, applied to overstretched caregivers.

Alice's Exhaustion

Alice reached the point of complete exhaustion. She felt utterly depleted and disenchanted with her career. She couldn't shake the constant chattering in her mind from a voice that critiqued her every thought and blamed her for everything. "Why have I allowed myself to become so consumed and exhausted with my work? Why has my dream job turned out to be so disappointing? Were my expectations too high? Is it just my immature idealism that keeps me wanting more? If I was meant for this career, then why am I feeling so disconnected?"

Yet every time she contemplated a change in her situation, the same familiar ghosts came around saying, "Don't push your luck, you have a good job and good benefits. You still have student loans to pay off. You need to provide for your family. Stay in your role. Everyone else seems able to. Your colleagues will think you're crazy. This was your dream; you just had a false sense of what it would be like."

Alice's days were filled with repetitive tasks and routines. The only changes she could see coming were going to make things worse. She felt so numb that she could barely remember, let alone feel, any desire to serve others. Though she had seen this reaction in her colleagues, she didn't expect it in herself. At first she thought she just needed a vacation, but she slowly realized the type of fatigue she had wasn't going to be cured by a good night's sleep, a day off, or even a month in Maui.

Alice sensed a rapidly progressing personal case of chronic fatigue syndrome. She knew from talking to other colleagues that feelings of professional emptiness would inevitably follow. Sure enough, she soon began noticing her jealousy of the janitor's job or other occupations that have set hours and nothing to do with healthcare or even with people. She began to feel more and more defeated.

Alice had the typical progression. At first, she was unable to fully put into words what she was experiencing. Frequently, burnout begins with a disillusioned, exhausted feeling we can't really wrap our minds around. Soon disassociation and emotional disconnection from ourselves and others surfaces.

There then follows a cul-de-sac of recurrent questioning or complaining— repeating the same story over and over.

Take the story of another nurse whose monologue may sound familiar.

"I am so burned out on talking to families, especially when I have a second patient to take care of. I now prefer taking care of a sedated post-op baby. The parents are not allowed to visit until the baby is stable and you don't have a second critical patient to attend to. I was never like that before. I always loved family interaction. I would encourage parents at my bedside and the adrenalin rush of having another crucially ill patient would nurture the side of me that loves a challenge. But now, I am so exhausted that I don't even want to talk to people, let alone prepare them for discharge while worrying about another patient."

Often, we do not take the time to peel back the layers to really see our current state. We get so caught up in the business of life that we forget to take an inventory of where we are in our job satisfaction. Below are some questions that might identify where you fall on the spectrum of burn out.

Self-Assessment	Always	No	Sometimes
Do I dread going to work?			
Am I frequently irritated with co-workers?			
Am I frequently bored with assignments?			
Does boredom and dissatisfaction increase year after year?			
Do I resent having to listen to other people's problems since mine feel just as distressing?			
Has professionalism replaced my compassion?			
Have I become more cynical and sarcastic?			
Do I spend time with others at work in the safety of a collective cynicism?			
Do I have compassion fatigue?			
Am I too drained to mobilize any passion?			

Do I have any energy to share with anyone else?			
Do I feel trapped in my job?			
Do I wish I had other options?			
Do I feel detached and disconnected from the relationships that could nurture my personal growth?			
Do I feel as if I'm just surviving instead of thriving?			

Grieving Our Loss

If you answered "Always" or "Sometimes" to the majority of those questions, that is a sign of serious dissatisfaction, or burnout. However, it is also an opportunity. It is a sign that you're being called to care for the patient within yourself.

If you choose to ignore burnout, this rich potential of healing ourselves gets eclipsed by deeper and deeper apathy. But, accepted for what it is, burnout can also lead to a rare, new chance to focus the healing energy you usually give to others onto yourself.

Burnout is a time of grief, and we only grieve what we love. In this case, we grieve the loss of the passion that once motivated us. We grieve for the way stress and job dissatisfaction have adversely affected our connections with our patients and colleagues. The grief in burnout mirrors the classic stages one goes through when grieving other sorts of losses: denial, anger, bargaining, depression, and acceptance. But in burnout, these stages rarely occur in a linear fashion.

To deny exploration of our grief is to deny the emotional and spiritual healing that is being evoked within us. Instead of denying, we can choose to clean out our thoughts the way a grieving widow cleans out the closets after her husband's death. She doesn't unceremoniously dump his things in the trash as if it weren't inherently linked to her life and history. To the contrary, she goes through all of the clothes and the memorabilia, dealing with all of it *slowly*, consciously deciding what is worth saving and savoring. As we grieve, we too must contemplate what needs to be let go and what needs to be protected. The slowed-down energy of grief can be quite healing. It takes us out of life's swift current and allows us time to sort out our thoughts.

A Doorway to Transformation

Burnout can be an exquisite opportunity for discovery. Embraced and accepted, it can jump-start a journey of personal transformation. Our current medical model has the healer's energy solely directed toward a patient. Had we been trained in some other tradition, we might have been taught that an essential part of being a healer includes achieving a balance between personal and professional wholeness. We would have been taught to align our spirit in such a way as to share ourselves without diminishing our true nature.

While we weren't taught that, burnout can direct us to a model in which the healer realizes his or her own need for healing. Fully accepting what is really going on inside of us draws us into an inner experience that is the beginning for our healing. It takes deep love and respect for the self to stay with this process. In fact, it takes the *same* love and respect we give to our patients.

To experience and understand the suffering of others, Buddhists say, we need to deal with our own suffering. Burnout pulls us into that suffering. It pulls us into a still point in our career life, and that can be a gift that expands our compassion as a caregiver. The Buddhist mantra for this is, "May my suffering show me the way to compassion."

Once we develop a willingness to accept our suffering for what it is instead of denying it, we move into a place where we can access some real data about our situation. Not the type of technical data that we currently honor in healthcare, but subjective data. This subjectivity is a form of self-auscultation. As with detecting heart murmurs, it takes time, practice, and experience to master this skill.

Our personal suffering can be a great resource for discovering the deeper connections between ourselves and our patients. If we listen to the symptoms of burnout, we begin to realize there is something new trying to be born within us—a new relationship with ourselves and our role. As we cultivate our interior life, compassion and wisdom will flourish in a way that will enhance our jobs.

Healthy Selfishness

Burnout can be a time for transformation from a tired identity to one that recaptures our original intentions in medicine. If appropriately addressed, burnout's discomfort elicits introspection and reflection into our lives. We can look at burnout as a still point in our career. A contemplative pause brought on by our angst or boredom, but a pause worth exploring. Perhaps burnout is a transformation that is an evolutionary necessity for us to deepen and grow in our career path. It can be a great opportunity to stretch beyond our current capacities, to expand our thinking, to reexamine our values and priorities, and to change the perspective with which we see our careers. In short, this is a time for healthy selfishness. For some, burnout can be the best thing that can happen in their professional lives. Burnout can, and should, signal that we need to reassess our career situation.

Yet self-inquiry can be a tricky practice. You must have an accurate sense of where you are. In contemplating the following questions, remember that the more truthful you answer, the richer the opportunity that will be uncovered. Some of the questions may take you back to medical or nursing school, or even your first professional job. Others may touch on issues you have already been mulling over. Take some time to think about the following questions and, if you can, discuss them with a trusted colleague.

Self-Assessment

• What gives me energy in my work day? What drains my energy?

_____

_____

_____

• What conferences do I attend regardless of Continuing Education Units? What patients or family meetings do I willingly skip lunch to support?

_____

_____

• What causes me to disengage?

_____

_____

• What gifts do I possess that aren't currently allowed expression at work? What parts of myself can't show up or aren't used maximally?

_____

_____

_____

• What are my golden handcuffs? What material things in my life own me and keep me imprisoned? What keeps me a slave to my current endeavor?

_____

_____

• On what days last week did I come home drained and tired? On what days did I come home energized? What caused the difference?

_____

- What is the difference between *healthy* and *unhealthy* giving?

- What could I do to better maintain a healthy, balanced life outside my professional role? What is preventing me from doing that?

Thinking deeply about these questions can be thought of as a mental clean-up exercise.

Creating a Space

We are poised for change once we recognize that we don't need to settle for the strictly material, financial rewards our jobs offer and that our deeper, personal need for meaning and purpose is a vital part of the reason we're in healthcare.

Those who've been through burnout, and listened to what it had to teach them, are grateful for the experience. Like cancer patients who surprise us with their appreciation for their disease, we gain new understanding because we're challenged. In times of burnout, questions about life's meaning rise to the top of the list as they do with a diagnosis of cancer. Burnout is life creating a space for personal development, something a static role cannot do. Traveling through the process of burnout can be a deep, internal healing process.

Collective Burnout

Just as we have individual burnout, we can also have collective burnout. Healthcare seems to be even more burned out than any of the individual caregivers within it. Our collective burnout is trying to tell us something truly significant about our profession. Just as an individual can progress after burnout, so too can the healthcare industry's collective burnout mark the beginning of the next stage of medicine's evolution. Evolution occurs when a system breaks down and comes back to heal itself. It usually returns with something never envisioned before the breakdown. This burnout can also help us become more conscious drivers of the evolutionary potential in medicine by challenging us to continually envision and create a new paradigm. Just as we need time individually for self-care and development, the collective of healthcare needs the same.

Becoming Students of Life

It is important that we realize our potential. Personal transformation is not just about our needs or desires. It is also about the patient's needs or desires, as the following example shows.

Mark's Persistent Questioning

Mark's father had been ill a long time but finally was diagnosed with stage four glioblastoma multiforme—a nearly universally fatal brain tumor. Not being in the medical field, Mark and his family were naturally upset and filled with so many dark forebodings that they preferred to focus on the trivial instead—baseball games, last summer's family picnic, the antics of young nephews and nieces. Burned out on bad news, most of the relatives were chatting about TV shows or planned vacations when the team of surgeons entered the room.

Dead silence was cut by Mark's question to the head surgeon, "Sir, could you tell me the prognosis given his condition?" To which the surgeon replied, "We don't really give a prognosis in this situation."

As the surgeons left the room, Mark's family all returned to their previous conversations. Mark, one of the younger men in the family and not usually a leader within that group, nonetheless got up and followed the surgical team down the hallway. He realized he would have to ask his question in some other fashion. He searched to find some common ground with the physicians. Because they were men of science, he thought maybe if he asked about statistics he might get a clearer answer.

Taking a deep breath to try to calm his nerves, Mark confronted the surgeon eye-to-eye and sought to restate his question in a way he hoped might elicit a more definitive answer. "Sir, could you tell me the statistics on this type of tumor?" With that, the surgeon very matter-of-factly said, "Oh, 98 percent mortality within eleven months."

Mark returned to the room with a new awareness. He decided to immediately drop out of school in order to spend time with his father and to care for him. He tried to get his family to hear the raw statistics, but they seemed more at ease within the comfort zone of their denial.

That night, when visiting hours ended, Mark's family left but he stayed. The nurse came in to request that he leave, but he insisted that he didn't want to leave his father post-op with the possibility of the father waking at night, alone and in pain and pondering his prognosis. The kind nurse chose to look past the rules.

Mark was surprised how, in a situation like this, something came out of him that he hadn't expected. He'd become the caregiver—the protector. He became his father's father. Eschewing burnout, he had been totally transformed—a transformation he never regretted.

Mark questioned the conventions and was touched and changed by the experience. For healthcare workers and lay caregivers like Mark, the healer isn't separated from the healing taking place. Having to participate in a medical crisis of another often pulls hidden talents from within us. We, like Mark, need to let our roles and our ego drop. We become students of life in a new way as the caregiver joins the patient in this opportunity for growth.

Reconnection

Burnout is an opportunity to dive deep within oneself and truly examine who we are beneath our profession, our role, our identity, and our behavior. If we actively listen, we'll hear that we're being beckoned to call upon a future that will be spiritually, emotionally, physically, mentally, and clinically fresh. It can be vigorous and visionary on all levels—personally, professionally, and collectively.

After we have deeply examined the causes of our burnout and experienced the grief process, the time is right to assess, affirm, prune, discern, shift, change, grow, refresh our vision, and recommit. The key to transforming burnout is finding its message and then transforming ourselves by embracing an expanded sense of wholeness. Those who find their way through burnout's maze can reconnect with their creativity and their ideals.

Chapter 2
Who Squeezed the Soul from Our Workplace?

"No problem can be solved from the same level of consciousness that created it."

—Albert Einstein

A few decades ago, television usually characterized physicians as kindly father figures who spent time with their patients, gently dispensing both medicine and wisdom, with a nurse at his side holding the patient's hand. Think *Marcus Welby, M.D.*

By contrast, look at television's depiction of physicians and nurses today. Shows such as *E.R.* depict overworked, underappreciated caregivers struggling with professional and personal crises in a fast-paced, high-tech, urban hospital. How has medicine changed so drastically in such a short time? What has happened? External pressures exert such an influence on us that we often do not feel that we are in the occupation we originally signed up for. To reclaim our own power as a profession, we are going to have to get past the vague, disempowering sense that something beyond our control is happening.

This chapter will review some of the biggest, most recurrent complaints about how the joy of a job in the healthcare industry has been lost. We will also seek to show how our lack of deep self-examination keeps us from realizing our power to change this.

Additionally, we will demonstrate how we have been active participants in the problems affecting healthcare, not just victims of the outside influences of law and business. When we blame others, we tend to give away our power and lose the ability to pause and assess our own actions. As Viktor Frankl, a doctor and Holocaust survivor, wrote, "Everything can be taken from a man but ... the last of the human freedoms is to choose one's attitude in any given set of circumstances, to choose one's own way."

The Need for Diagnosis

As professionals, we are aware of the need for a thorough diagnosis before beginning treatment—quoted often as "A problem well defined is half solved." If we are honest, what we find when we look at medicine is that some of the outside influences have been controlled by us, some we have not yet sought to control, and others are indeed outside of our control. So we need to invoke the Serenity Prayer and ask ourselves, how do we affect the things we can change and honor those things we cannot? It is important to work on the former instead of getting caught up in the energy drain of the latter. We are stuck because we have focused on things that we cannot really influence.

Power Loss

As we shall see in this chapter, the healthcare profession has given its power away. How? By abdicating our power though apathy and inaction. We like to complain, for instance, about how law made big inroads into medicine as malpractice grew to be a huge issue. But the truth is, by not self-policing the incompetents among us, we invited the incursion. Similarly, while we may have recoiled at the notion of government coming in to regulate hours for residents, for decades we did nothing to change the onerous schedules and draconian routines that sapped the energy and clouded the attitudes of our young professionals. We, as well as our patients, rail—and rightfully so—against the cost-centric nature of medicine. But for years we were collectively cavalier about costs, ordering tests and buying equipment without any regard for the discipline of the bottom line.

On issue after issue, decade after decade, our victimized retelling of our collective story tends to leave out the part about how we left the door ajar so that the vandals could come in. In fact, we practically commanded them to take control. What we imagine was done *to* us was really done *by* us.

From psychiatry rotations, we are all familiar with patients who come in week after week with the same complaint. They are stuck in the same story. Trying to get them to see some self-culpability often is impossible. Similarly in healthcare, complaints about the system, whether voiced in the break room or in medical conferences, have not changed all that much over the years. Usually these complaints make healthcare workers the good cops in the story and the outside influences become the bad cops.

In this scenario, self-culpability is missed by the sheer redundancy of story. Tell a story often enough and it becomes *your* truth even if it is not *the* truth. In this next section, we are not so interested in what is true, personally or universally, but what is helpful. What perspective will help us reignite the professional engagement that we once had?

Here is our choice: We can continue to act like victims, unaware of how we influenced some of our deepest difficulties, or we can take responsibility for our part in those changes and become architects in the creation of a new vision for medicine's future.

Looking Anew at Our "Stories"

To open up a place for new understanding, we must learn to look at our stories in a different way. We need to be aware of our relationship to our problems. That is more powerful than the blame game. We are going to have to retell the stories while focusing on our own culpability in order to see what we might have done to encourage an external intrusion.

How did we get into the current predicament of the doctors and nurses as they are portrayed on television's *E.R.*? Whether you are a doctor, a nurse, an acupuncturist, a massage therapist, or an energy healer, the role you fill is part of the long and evolving development of the healing arts. We both create and are molded by the system we work in.

Our Evolution

In the nineteenth and early twentieth centuries, doctors traveled (often because they were the only ones with transportation) to the villages and farms where their patients lived. Treating patients at home allowed doctors to see them in their own surroundings. This helped put a patient's illness in the context of his or her living conditions and family dynamics. In times of severe crisis, the physician administered to the emotional as well as the physical needs of the family, filling the dual role of doctor and minister. In times of serious illness, it was not uncommon for doctors or nurses to stay with families of the sick, sleeping in their home and sharing their meals, acting as a trusted friend and a witness to their lives. This type of intimate relationship was the model many patients came to expect from their healthcare provider and often was also the quality of relationship that healthcare workers expected to share with their patients.

Fast-forward to our current situation. With nearly every job change, there is a change in healthcare plans. Patients change physicians more frequently than they change cars. Patients rarely see the same nurse if they are in the hospital for a few days recovering from an illness or procedure. The long-term devotion and awareness that a doctor or nurse might have had with his or her patient is gone, and with it, the depth and richness of that connection, an important cornerstone of healing, has been lost. Medicine has lost touch with its soul because the connection and interpersonal context have been misplaced.

How did we, as a profession, contribute to the loss of this dynamic? We can blame the insurance carriers or the highly mobile society we live in. Those are certainly both factors. But let's not forget to ask what we did as a profession that contributed to this loss of relationship. That is probably the only aspect of the situation we can influence.

Law Arrives

The '60s and '70s are now often called "the golden years of medicine" because of the physicians' fat paychecks. But if you talk to retired doctors who were working then, and if they are honest, they will tell you that some physicians did not always practice up to professional standards. When a doctor did something that might be seen as malpractice, his or her colleagues generally looked the other way. This unaddressed incompetence was the profession's dirty little secret.

Describing the climate of the time, one doctor recalled, "Physicians in those days were regarded with such respect they were almost considered infallible by the public. At that time there was so much ego in medicine. Physicians were given credit and took credit for much more than they were due. I remember wondering, When is this ball going to drop? We know from politics that it isn't long before someone who takes credit for good things gets blamed for the bad. As an obstetrician, though, I felt humbled, I was more of a minor assistant in a major miracle, but my patients seemed to feel otherwise, often giving me nearly complete credit for a normal pregnancy and delivery.

"But taking credit, undeserved as it may have been, for so long, we had to know that blame was going to follow. With accepting all this credit coupled with our lack of effective proctoring of our peers, we almost begged the legal system's intervention. To me it was like a patient not taking care of her health—run down, exhausted, smoking a pack a day, and then being surprised when cancer enters the picture. Because we didn't properly take care of the things we needed to take care of in our profession, we opened the door for the legal system to begin its own method of policing doctors, nurses, and hospitals. Then our profession began to act like victims of the litigious culture that has evolved. Looking back, we were really the neglectful architects of the situation."

As a result, few doctors were reported for problems in patient management. Our failure at self-policing created a vacuum. Rushing to fill that vacuum was a wave of aggressive lawyers with malpractice complaints, creating a climate of fear that rippled through all layers of healthcare. Medical practice changed from a model based on nurturance to a model based on fear. Physicians now began ordering test after test just to cover their butts. Monitoring and documentation became a priority.

Nurses bore the brunt of this change. One nurse said of that time: "I went into a delightfully humanistic profession and over a few years something changed and I was suddenly drowning in documentation. Overnight, it seemed as if caring for the chart was as important as caring for the patient. Eventually, my job devolved into task-oriented, role-defined, technologically based encounters that became mind- and heart-numbing in their monotonous uniformity. I rarely got to focus on any sort of relationship with the patient. My exciting job, which always impressed people at cocktail parties, had in fact become quite uninteresting and boring. True connection with my patients was sacrificed at the altar of efficiency."

The Business Invasion
The increasing legal emphasis was not the only big change affecting the healthcare environment. Business issues also rose to the forefront. After the time of the house-call physician, doctors began expanding their own offices. They then had to attend to the demands of owning and operating a business as well as being a healthcare provider. The dual role of doctor/businessman meant less time with patients and more time focused on business concerns. New physicians now are often shocked by these demands.

As one resident said: "I was so surprised at what my training didn't prepare me for. After getting my first job, I ended up in frequent lunchtime and after-hour meetings discussing hiring new staff, credentialing doctors, wrestling with insurance and billing issues, retirement plans, medical-record demands, and office-investment opportunities. I was so unfamiliar with these issues that instead of my patients dominating my life and thoughts, these new issues demanded an inordinate amount of my attention. I felt like I'd lost my center."

In fact, we collectively lost our center several decades ago. We were out of our league in allowing ourselves to become preoccupied with business matters, which, in truth, most of us do not do very well. We might have created a new type of position to handle business matters or come up with some other creative solution. But, in large measure, we tried to handle business matters as well as the medical ones and both suffered. The result? Business came in to take over medicine in the form of Health Maintenance Organizations (HMOs) and managed care.

A retired physician stated: "I'm not surprised that businessmen started to look at healthcare with a profit motive. The profits available seemed quite evident and became even more obvious as monies lost in lawsuits were publicized. The rising cost of health coverage placed an increasing financial burden on industry, inviting businesspeople to start looking at our field with a level of financial responsibility that we as healthcare providers didn't always honor or even recognize.

"As business interests encroached, it seemed that almost overnight the medical culture went from ordering excessive tests for legal protection, to protocol-based interventions aimed at using the least resources possible. HMOs were created to ensure financial efficiency and reduce healthcare costs. This goal seemed to become paramount, dominating our interface with patients. The 'time is money' paradigm of the business world began to become integrated into healing encounters."

In fact, as one resident commented, "You were taught to be so efficient that if you spent more than five minutes with a patient you were seen as wasting time." Giving enough time to listen to patients with the intention of true connection was no longer encouraged.

Cost-effectiveness dictated larger patient loads for nurses as well as shorter clinic-visit times for physicians. As a nurse stated, "The larger my patient load, the less the hospital spends on staffing, but this leaves me with little time for patient interaction. Medicine evolved into a business compensating healthcare providers for their efficiency and devaluing many of the qualities, like patience and compassion, that used to make a job in healthcare so fulfilling."

As the time spent on patients declined, not surprisingly, those patients began to feel uncared for. The new business model stole something significant from the humanity of healthcare. Healthcare providers were trained to call their patients "customers" or "clients." As bottom-line efficiency and profits began to dominate the field, medicine lost touch with its soul.

A hospice nurse shared her perspective: "In my career, medicine has totally transformed. The solo practitioner I used to work for as well as the Catholic charity hospital where I put in overtime are now both paradigms that are almost extinct. When I ask myself, from my current perspective as a hospice nurse, 'How did this happen?' or 'What could we have done to change this?' I can only think that maybe as healthcare providers we were negligent about a focus we should have embraced all along.

"Medicine is a field that is so emotionally laden. It's not the same as business, but maybe we are partly to blame for not taking care of what needed to be cared for on some level. There was an interesting statistic that something like 40 percent of healthcare dollars are spent in the last four days of someone's life. Who is to blame for this? Ask any group of people, healthcare workers included, 'How many of you want to die in a hospital?' Rarely does a hand go up.

"Maybe if we could have learned the hospice consciousness sooner, maybe if we could have been more in touch with and honored our own limitations, we could have developed better internal guidelines around extending life and resource utilization, instead of having to have outside influences such of politics and business come to dominate our decision making."

Scientification

Medicine had to accommodate both the stranglehold of the legal system and the constraints of the business model. Balancing risk management and cost-efficiency isn't always easy. Along with its growing business concerns, medicine also moved more and more in the direction of science. Struggling with these issues led to the current paradigm that we call evidence-based medicine, or EBM. EBM is frequently spoken of with the evangelical fervor of something new, but this model of practice is not yet maturely integrated into healthcare. Medicine has always been based on the best available data, and science has always been one pillar of good medicine. Certainly most of us are proud of our advances in science, but is medicine merely applied science? Unlike the times of the house-call doctor, randomized studies and statistics now take precedence over experience and intuition. A solitary pillar does not hold up a building.

Conflating Medicine with Science

As one physician said, "The new outcome-based dialogue was, it seemed to me, a cover for an inquiry into the balance between cost and efficacy."

The old paradigm of each patient being unique took too much time and was hardly efficient; now we use statistically acquired patient-based outcomes. Research-based treatment was rarely structured around a particular patient and became targeted to generalized disease categories. This research-based practice evolved into EBM. This seems the epitome of conflating clinical medicine with science.

This sort of practice and thinking has unintended consequences. We know all too well that it is possible to define an outcome of scientific activity (the prolongation of life) without referring to its humanistic aspect (the quality of living and quality of dying). The problem is the removal of the second pillar of the healthcare system—the rich, human interactions and spiritual component.

Medicine has become highly efficient using the evidence-based model. But the tradeoff has been the loss of connection between healthcare providers and patients. And this disconnection is not just with our patients. We have developed rigid patterns of relating on all levels of interaction—personally, professionally, and collectively. The disconnect that we feel with our patients and co-workers has led us into a psychologically and emotionally stunted workplace.

Government's Role

Just as we seemingly invited the incursion of law and business into our field, we have done the same with government by not being proactive and taking care of matters within our control. The ridiculously long hours and bizarre work schedules we imposed on our young professionals was a source of rueful mirth—a tawdry badge of honor passed along from one generation to the next. We knew it, we saw it, but we did not act on it. Is it any wonder the government had to come in and regulate something that everyone knew was ridiculous?

Until recently, it was expected that a resident's training required a 110-hour work week. This had been the pattern in medical training for decades and the profession saw no reason to change this practice despite the atmosphere of increased litigation. The nurse who was revered was the one who had worked the most overtime, and many of these hours were tacked onto a twelve-hour shift. Once again we should ask ourselves: What did we neglect that let outside sources influence our profession so radically?

It took government intervention to mandate a legal limit to the number of hours a resident can work without being considered fatigued. To think that a caring group of souls, most of whom had gone through the same system, did not change this military-style regimen on their own is fairly unbelievable. It is a good illustration of our ability to be stuck in a recurrent story from generation to generation without making the obvious changes needed.

Such blindness to what is right in front of us recalls a fable about a homeless man who sat, every day, on a discarded crate on the side of a boulevard and asked each passerby for some change. Some averted their gaze, others awkwardly muttered, "Sorry, I don't have any change." But almost every day, one man told the beggar, "Why don't you look in the box you are sitting on?" Days and weeks passed until, finally, the homeless man decided to stand up and look inside the crate. He found it filled with gold.

In healthcare, we have been sitting on our crates, unaware of how we have participated in our circumstances and equally unaware of the gold that lies inside each of us and in our profession.

What Can We Do?

Alienation occurs when contemporary healthcare providers feel that what drives medicine no longer drives them. These incursions by medicine, law, business, and government are a big part of the reason healthcare workers feel alienated. As a result, some healthcare workers are consumed by stress, others by boredom, some are lost in the frenzy of *doing*, and still others are lost in fatigue. We find ourselves in a collective depression, unable to believe our circumstances will be any different, let alone that we can do anything to change them.

But once we realize that we have been unconscious participants in the recurrent pattern of changes in healthcare, the light bulb in our minds may switch on. Once we do become conscious of our unintended neglect of some things, the question becomes: What can we do with this new awareness?

First, healthcare providers must take ownership of, and responsibility for, the collective condition of medicine. Instead of focusing on feeling victimized by the legal system, the business paradigm, the scientific mono-focus, or any other future superimposed constructs, we must take responsibility for the dynamics that keep us stuck.

Second, we are going to have to change our workplace conversations. To do this we have to learn how to first hear, and then tell, a different story about our situation. From this new story, fresh questions will evolve.

Fresh Questions

Among the questions we should be asking ourselves:
- Can we take medicine on its own path of healing?
- What new philosophy of medicine can we embrace that will allow a transformation of the context in which we currently function?
- Can we evolve a more compassionate interpersonal responsiveness not only for our patients, but for ourselves, our co-workers, and the needs of healthcare?
- How do we create space for the emotional and spiritual evolution of healthcare?
- What is a new model we can look to?

It is also important to ask: With all that has changed in healthcare, what has stayed the same? The *patient* has stayed the same. If we stay grounded in that relationship, we will find what brought us into healthcare in the first place.

Further, we must realize that healthcare entails not only healing patients, but healing ourselves. Such perspective presents a larger context for our work, infusing a creative healing energy that gives us permission for continual growth instead of stagnation. Once we start this growth on a personal level, we reestablish the fundamental grounding needed to heal healthcare. When we enlarge our ideas of who we are and what we can be to each other, the system, and ourselves, we create an opportunity to grow.

This new perspective may involve fresh responses. The true voice of healthcare has been silenced, but we can still hear that voice inside our hearts if we embrace a more personal and a more spiritual perspective. In fact, engaging in such a deeply personal shift in consciousness might be our only option in the face of a system that seems unfixable by any other means. To retrieve the spiritual foundation in healthcare is the collective homework of our time.

Chapter 3
What Is Keeping Us Stuck?

"Something we were withholding made us weak, until we found it was ourselves."
—Robert Frost

As healthcare professionals, we arrive for a day of work as individuals with unique personal histories and personalities. We hold within us our likes and dislikes, talents, skills, hopes, dreams, and fluctuating moods. Yet, as we walk into the healthcare setting, we become part of a collective experience in an environment shaped by group identity and group beliefs. The consciousness generated by the collective consists largely of what everyone agrees about—what is considered appropriate and inappropriate, true and untrue, important or of slight value.

Basically, we check our individuality at the door when we step into a healthcare setting. The collective creates a group mind-set with a powerful ability to shape our behavior. Caught in this collective experience, we become stuck in patterns of relating and working that squeeze out variety in our human experience. When this variety is squeezed out of our experience, our ability to grow and evolve is deeply wounded.

In chapter 2, we saw how the collective experience in healthcare was affected by external influences and our reactions to them. In this chapter, we will look at some of the internal workplace dynamics that tend to keep us stuck.

The Cost of Accommodation
Deep-seated patterns occur when we are tethered to a collective agreement. Group thinking impacts all aspects of how we work—from our role definitions

to our work ethic, from our status in the medical hierarchy to the way we communicate. This results in a collective blindness because ideas and assumptions become conditioned into fixed ways of interacting and being. "Accommodating to the collective is safer and on some levels certainly easier," Nietzsche commented, "but the personal cost is tremendous."

Forgoing our individuality in order to concede to the collective is like being in a large family that tries to appease all its members when planning a vacation. The parents will not say they want to go to the beach and the kids will not insist on the theme park. Trying to please everyone, the family ends up spending a weekend camped out in the backyard. All are participating in a type of collective mind-set and everyone ends up unhappy.

Why does this dynamic exist? It's often simply the function of joining a collective, of which a family is the most familiar example. Just as our role in a family can force us to sacrifice essential pieces of our personality, this can also happen in nearly every collective experience. As we age and get more comfortable with our position, we begin to see the limitations of our roles. We grow but our roles remain the same.

Hindered from realizing our expanding potential, we end up camping in the backyard. We end up stuck with the limited self-expression and repetition the collective requires from our roles. When the tedium of our jobs makes us feel more like automatons than freethinking individuals, we become mired in boredom. Boredom makes us feel enslaved to the collective consciousness. We share the same complaints, but no one seems capable of the independent thinking required to escape the collective stagnation.

One nurse put it the following way. "My job has made me a machine. I am serious. I am literally an extension of the monitor. My job takes little thought and if I were to take time to think, I would perform slower than is expected. My efficiency is based on the fact that I work in a systematic way. I actually spend four hours of my day recording vitals. Over and over, day in and day out, it is so tedious and monotonous. It creates machine-like behavior.

"You lose a sense of yourself. It feels like you could be a robot and do the same thing. I find that when I leave work, I am still like a machine. Oh, don't get me wrong, I eventually slip out of it, but for the first few hours I am what I was at work. I find myself, more and more often, doing things in a mechanical manner.

"I used to picture my job as a job. Something I could do and then go home and live. You would be amazed at how difficult that is. A job isn't something you leave when your shift is over. It is something that stays with you all day."

As healthcare workers caught in the collective, we become attached to, and perpetuate, attitudes, beliefs, behaviors, and outcomes that allow us to be safe and accepted in the group. Often, our collective agreement restricts our responses and actions to a limited few.

The Crab Catcher's Story

In New England waters, crab catchers line the bottom of their boats with coffee cans. As crabs are caught, they are placed two to a can. As long as two crabs are together in each coffee can, the crab catchers never need to put a lid on the can. A single crab will climb out, but when two are together, they pull on each other and neither can escape.

The crabs are victims of their own behavior because they cannot learn to overcome their instinctive reaction. Our reactions also tend to come from reflex behaviors—redundant patterns of interacting which keep us stuck, if only by their repetitiveness. Our roles are a set of behaviors and actions that were standardized and ratified by the collective long before any of us put on a white coat or scrubs, picked up needles, or bought a bottle of massage oil.

With submission to these ill-fitting roles, we embrace the harmful patterns that the healthcare collective generates. These are holding patterns which encourage stuck habits within the profession. We end up avoiding the discomfort that can be generated by a deeper inquiry, but in doing so we sacrifice the creativity that questions breed. We are trained to assess a situation from a role-based perspective.

We Know

"Look, here they come," Marion said as she nudged Pamela's shoulder. Pamela raised her eyes from the report she was filling out and saw a group of young nurses following closely behind the director of nursing. "So wide-eyed and innocent," Pamela said shaking her head. "Want to make a bet on how many will drop out within the first year?"

Marion laughed. "It doesn't matter to me." She opened her desk drawer and pulled out a picture of a palm tree swaying in the breeze on a sandy beach. "I'm one year away from no more doctors talking to me like I don't know what I am doing, no more filling out the same incident report six times, and no more being called 'nurse' or 'hey' instead of by my name."

Unlike crabs in a coffee can, we have the ability to free ourselves from collective behavior by asserting our individual natures. We need to learn to create space for ourselves within the collective so that we may observe how we cope with its positive and negative aspects. This spaciousness will help us to take control of our professional environment instead of becoming controlled by it.

Unfortunately for Pamela and Marion, they have neither tried nor been taught how to create space for themselves within the collective. Nurse Marion ran through a litany of complaints about her job—being talked down to, filling out multiple reports, and losing the identity connected to her title and role. She accepted these complaints as just the way things are. Instead of trying to change her own reality, she looked forward to retiring to a vacation destination. Marion saw no opportunity for change in the system. When we are totally immersed in the drama of our workplace, we cannot gain the perspective and distance to observe our situation objectively. An entrenched and stagnant belief system cannot be evaluated when we are so locked in.

We Become Our Roles

Whether a doctor, nurse, radiology technician, phlebotomist, acupuncturist, massage therapist, or naturopath, we all felt we had unique abilities and talents that we could contribute to healthcare. But little by little, the role, even if ill-fitting, became our identity at work. This pattern not only limits the individuality of the healthcare worker, but can limit our understanding of the patient as well. Thus, patients come to be defined by the disease they have—the patient in Room 202 is the "coronary bypass." Healthcare professionals are defined by the disease they treat—the nurse who takes care of the "coronary" is the "cardiac nurse" and the physician who attends the "coronary patient" is the "heart surgeon." The typical healthcare worker ends up lost in a crowd of workers who have given up their individual identities and are now labeled according to their educations, titles, or specialties.

Scratch the surface of a modern healthcare unit and any number of collective patterns becomes obvious.

Here are three additional patterns that you may be able to identify with or recognize:

Committing Ourselves to Imbalance. Being harried is practically a healthcare worker's badge of honor. Check your co-workers' holiday letters and see if being stupendously busy isn't something they seem to almost brag about. Frenetic energy is seen as a form of passion. We applaud the doctor who stays up all night and still handles his clinic the next day, or the nurse who works long hours of overtime. The same is true of the self-sacrificing alternative practitioners who see patients long into the evening hours, squeeze them into lunch breaks, and often accommodate them with home visits without any compensation for travel time.

If anyone approaches his or her job with a quiet calmness, others may assume they must not really care about their work. If they are not in a hurry, busy, or tired, they must not be committed. Those who follow the collective status quo are valued, despite the fact that the status quo sustains imbalance and leads to an unhealthy workforce.

Dr. Stan's Story

Dr. Stan worked long hours in the OR. In fact, he worked more overtime than the other doctors, carried the largest caseload, and performed the most procedures. Dr. Stan also served as chairperson of the hospital's ethics committee. At the annual awards banquet, none of Dr. Stan's co-workers were surprised that he was honored as "Doctor of the Year."

As Dr. Stan stood on the podium to accept the award, he looked at his wife and son sitting in the audience and he realized this awards banquet was the first time they had eaten dinner together as a family in a month. He looked at the plaque with his name engraved on it and wondered if the hours spent at the hospital and this communal recognition were worth the time spent away from his family. He also wondered if he knew how to slow down.

We are trained to anticipate a job that creates imbalance. We sacrifice time for ourselves and our loved ones for the sake of our profession. We routinely expect ourselves and each other to be imbalanced and exhausted. We acquiesce to the chronic energy depletion that comes from long hours at work. We accept the sleeplessness and time away from our personal lives as a natural consequence of our jobs.

The imbalance that our job forces upon us and our families is also felt by our patients and co-workers. Dr. Stan and many physicians and nurses like him spend such little time with so many different patients that if they saw them the next day on the street, they would not recognize them. This lack of connection seems crucial to sustaining the pace of what could be called robotic medicine.

We have gotten ourselves into a position where we shift quickly from one acute case to another, never having time to shed the stress and emotions of the first. This pattern can be toxic because of what it does not let us see. We are too busy to investigate other options in the way we work and interact with others.

Accepting an Antiquated Hierarchy. Another pattern that seems as old as our collective is the medical hierarchy. The hierarchical structure and the status of roles in the healthcare collective are antiquated compared to what is being embraced in other professions. Businesses, and even the military, have learned that strict top-down leadership is limiting because there is simply too much to know for the few in power to make the best decisions. Even so, doctors still write orders, often with little collaboration from other team members.

Doctor's Orders

A doctor was very upset that an order she had written had not been properly carried out. On morning rounds, she turned to the nurses and said in a very angry tone, "What part of this don't you understand? These are called doctor's orders for a reason; they are not suggestion boxes."

The hierarchy is dysfunctional when you hear stories like the classic nurse's dilemma, "Do I wake up the patient to give him this sleeping pill?"

Often, we see nurses accepting and supporting the maintenance of hierarchy. Some tend to manipulate the traditional doctor/nurse relationship instead of trying to improve it.

A Preceptor's Story

As a preceptor, Nurse Kim was training a new nurse in the ICU and began discussing communication with doctors. Kim explained the art of making suggestions to some of the physicians to her orientee. "Dr. Roberts does not take recommendations well from nurses, so you have to put your suggestions in the form of a question to preserve his superiority." She added, "Dr. Davis gets really quiet and he withdraws from the conversation when he's upset. If he starts looking sullen and doesn't say anything, you should just leave him alone for a while. Whatever you do, don't ask him any questions at that time." Finally, she warned, "Watch out for Dr. Seville, she's tricky. If she rushes in late and begins chatting endlessly about the drama of her personal life, that means she's extremely stressed and it is best to give her some time to settle into work before you can expect her at the bedside."

Nurse Kim and others like her do not recognize that their behavior supports the maintenance of an archaic, role-based hierarchy. They do not see how limiting it is and how energy draining it is to create receptivity in the other before they can have their suggestions heard.

Nurses have developed the art of role-based suggestion, obliquely offering various treatment options to the physician rather than acting collaboratively, as peer to peer. Nurse Kim maintains that such maneuvering, drawn from what she calls her "recipe box" of tactics, is the only way she can get what she needs for her patients while preserving a cordial relationship with some of the physicians.

Nurse Jane's Story

Nurse Jane noticed that her patient looked sicker by the minute, yet the lab results did not reflect her gut feeling. Jane did not want to question the lab results, so she kept her thought of oncoming sepsis to herself. She knew she had no empirical data to back up her gut feeling. Later, she noticed that the patient had developed a temperature. She asked the physician to order another set of labs. When the labs were drawn, the results revealed that the patient was septic.

Before reporting what she felt, Jane thought she needed to have the proper data to back up her intuition and convince the physician. Jane became bound to deep-seated collective patterns that stifled her behavior. When our actions are prescribed by our role, we end up with little ability to manifest unique, intuitive, and heartfelt responses to situations. If Jane worked in an environment where she felt encouraged to trust her intuition, she would have made sure her patient was started on antibiotics earlier. Instead, the nurse sensed that the collective would not value her intuition; so she waited and her patient got worse. After we have accrued some experience, our intuition should be honored as much as our intellect.

Requisite Sureness. The roles we play in a structured hierarchy clearly seem to suppress our openness to dialogue. As the next anecdote shows, we may be encouraging our physicians to develop an attitude of sureness, even when it is not appropriate.

Quick ... The Answer?

An attending physician conducting rounds asked an intern, "What is the normal white count for a newborn?" The intern immediately responded as if she was completely certain: "The range is 10,000 to 15,000." The numbers were incorrect, but the intern's tone of certainty was so remarkable that the attending asked her about her sureness.

Not surprised at all by the question, the intern explained very matter-of-factly, "Oh, I just finished a rotation at the military hospital and there it seemed to matter less if you were right about something than if you kept a confident demeanor when you responded to questioning."

When we follow roles without ever questioning them or looking deeper, we stop growing.

Becoming a Witness

Once we catch ourselves playing a role, our recognition creates a space between ourselves and our roles and we move into the position of a witness. Unlike the crabs, we gain a little spaciousness, we stand in the place of witnessing, we create a space for observation, and remain aware of what is going on in a situation without engaging in the familiar patterns of simple reaction.

Transformation can occur if we can bear witness to the negative and positive aspects of the healthcare collective. Once we see the collective dynamics for what they are, we can respond to our situation rather than merely react. Sometimes awareness of the problem is all that is required to solve it. Once we can look at collective patterns of behavior and thinking, and think outside of them, we can let another dimension of consciousness in. Free from blind acceptance of the collective norm, we can become an integral part of the real healing process. Although the modern healthcare collective falls short of the ideal, the potential exists to derive a great deal of good from groups of healthcare professionals working together to heal themselves and their patients.

It is vital that we learn to harness the positive power of the collective and subdue the negative aspects. We can do that by changing the way we think about our roles and our jobs. The consequences of considering roles more significant than the individuals who fill them can be very restrictive.

As we will see in the following chapters, it is primarily our relationship with ourselves that must grow and develop in order for us to repossess our unique individuality in our workplace. Each one of us must accept personal responsibility for our ongoing participation in collective patterns and activities. Collective change comes from changed individuals, not the other way around. Changed individuals can expand collective assumptions and create new group dynamics. From ourselves, this change spreads to our relationships with others—first, to those closest to us; then to our co-workers and patients; and finally to our interaction with the system at large. In other words, we have the power to re-create our experience in our profession, from the inside out.

In creating a different experience for ourselves, we can encourage healthcare to return to its original foundation.

Such exploration and deep questioning reveal a powerful potential beyond roles, beyond patterns and unspoken collective agreements. Religions speak of personal transcendence as the sense of being *in* the world, not *of* the world. For healthcare practitioners, the possibility of transcendence and change might be expressed as being *in* the role, not *of* the role, and it brings with it the possibility of discovering individuality right in the midst of the collective experience.

Part II: Treatment

Chapter 4
Cultivating Inner Development

"Human beings are not born once and for all on the day their mothers give birth to them, but ... life obliges them over and over again to give birth to themselves."
—Gabriel Garcia Marquez

To move past burnout, we must embark on a journey that has a different focus from what we learned in our training. The essential shift entails changing our focus from studying and healing others to studying and healing ourselves.

In this chapter, we will begin to study psychological concepts that we can integrate into our awareness to help expand our personal deepening. We will seek psychological and spiritual principles that will permit us to extend ourselves to others in a more healthy and spiritual manner. As we do this, we will begin to rediscover the soul of the healing artist within. What we particularly need to look at is what suppresses and what nurtures that soul.

Spotting Patterns in Others

It is often easy for caregivers to recognize repetitive behaviors in patients: Maybe Mr. Smith has high cholesterol because he overeats, Mrs. Frederick has emphysema because she smokes, and Mr. Peters gets headaches because he works long hours at a computer and rarely sleeps. For a healer, the link between a patient's behavior and his or her symptoms is frequently painfully obvious. If Mr. Smith, Mrs. Frederick, and Mr. Peters changed a few of their daily habits, their health and their lives would improve significantly. But our power to help them heal is limited by their ability or desire to follow medical advice and help heal themselves.

The solutions may seem obvious, yet patients often cannot or do not make the necessary changes. With a little psychological spelunking, we might find that Mr. Smith overeats because his mother cooked lavish dinners and made snacks for him when he was a young boy with the hope of consoling him during his parents' divorce. Food comforts him. Food feels like love. Maybe Mrs. Frederick found social acceptance when she started smoking with other teenagers. Smoking makes her feel confident and accepted. And Mr. Peters may overwork because of his distant father, who rarely showed him any attention except for acknowledging his good work in school. Work makes him feel like a lovable person.

No one can simply walk away from their patterns because often they have deeply integrated them into their subconscious habits. Patients lack the awareness to recognize the control these habits have over them. While Mr. Smith may remember his mother's cooking, he might not recognize why she cooked for him. Similarly, Mrs. Frederick and Mr. Peters most likely do not remember the specific events that led them to smoke and overwork. Their behavior patterns were developed so long ago that it's difficult to remember how they acquired them in the first place. While these patterns are easy to· spot in others, they are often less apparent in ourselves.

Repetition Compulsion
Sigmund Freud may be a bit past his prime, but his theory of repetition compulsion is still relevant. Using the idea behind his theory, we will see how patterning from an early age can show up in our work lives. Freud felt that humans are subconsciously drawn to re-create situations based on the most defining and dramatic experiences in their childhood. He believed that we do this time and time again to learn how to heal these traumatic experiences.

For example, when we find ourselves feeling as if someone is pushing our buttons, it is helpful to remember that, though someone *pushed* our buttons, they did not *install* those buttons. Instead, we may be reacting to a pattern set up in childhood. We can develop a better awareness of when this button was installed and a better understanding of the pattern instead of reacting reflexively to the person or situation that pushed it. To do this, we need to become aware of what is buried beneath our reactions, not just externalize the reaction by projecting blame on another.

Freud's theory of repetition compulsion can be compared to a computer. Despite all that a computer is capable of doing, if it is stuck continuously printing the first page it was ever programmed to print, not much of its potential can be realized. When we confront a situation similar to the experiences that marked our minds as children, our minds will print the same page, in the form of rote behavioral patterns, over and over again. Deprogramming these patterns requires, first, an awareness of the problem. It is not as easy to see the complex psychological patterns that determine our behavior as it is to open a user's manual for a computer and change the way it works. According to Freud, the mind will continue to print the same page until we learn to *remember, repeat, and work through* the experiences that trigger our behaviors.

Often, these patterns limit our self-expression to a few well-worn reactions that keep us from exploring and revealing ourselves as a whole person. This recurrent superficiality can keep us in the shallow end of life's pool, causing us to miss the opportunities to heal ourselves while we heal our patients. With some specific techniques, we can learn to recognize our unique behavior patterns and identify their source. Once these issues are uncovered, we can develop a healing awareness, an awareness that can be curative. We can become aware of our own psychological and emotional wounds and learn how they shape, define, and limit our interactions with others. And when we heal these wounds, we become better caregivers to our patients, ourselves, our co-workers, and our workplaces.

Workplace Interactions

The workplace is a wonderful place to confront our patterns and heal our wounds. In fact, our workplace interactions can be viewed as a form of social meditation, a form of contemplative practice with applications for healing both ourselves and our relationships. We do not want to overlook this opportunity.

The following story illustrates one healthcare worker's experience in confronting recurrent behavior patterns.

Relating in a New Way

Nurse Kathy was the consummate caregiver. In addition to her work as a Pediatric ICU nurse, she took foster children into her home. When a new teenage foster son, Ben, was placed with her, she moved him in, got him feeling comfortable, helped him get used to his new school, and hired tutors to help him with his schoolwork. Ben did better in school once he was in an environment where he could study. He made friends and seemed to enjoy his new home. But just as things settled into a peaceful routine, Ben started acting out. He got into trouble at school and started to turn minor situations into raging arguments at home. Kathy couldn't understand why Ben was suddenly so hard to get along with.

Her caseworker reminded her that Ben had a severely alcoholic father and recommended that Kathy read some of the literature on children of alcoholics. She learned that because Ben was raised in an alcoholic home, he spent his youth unable to predict which days would be good and which would be awful. When his father came home, he never knew if he would get a hug or a slug. Kathy realized that on a deep, unconscious level, this was the connection Ben was familiar with. The feeling of peace Kathy provided was unfamiliar and out of his comfort zone.

Ben needed drama and chaos to feel connected. Ben only knew what he knew. His sense of comfort, his sense of connection, was based on conflict and that's how he thought of love. Once Kathy realized this, it made sense that at first, when there was a lot of drama around a new home and new school, Ben was fine. But as soon as things got to where most people would feel comfortable, Ben couldn't feel connected, or at least the type of connection he was used to. Once Kathy understood that Ben's behavior was fairly stereotypic of a child of an alcoholic, this new awareness allowed her to help him learn to connect with people in a different way.

On a similar note, a few years back, a researcher found that about 60 percent of ICU and emergency room nurses identified themselves as adult children of alcoholics. Certainly many of these nurses, like Ben, bring unconscious dynamics to the workplace. We may be drawn into certain fields for various unconscious reasons. The chaos in the ICU and ER may be quite familiar and comfortable. One physician was overheard saying, "In our neonatal unit, the nurses are great when it is busy. They are so competent and thorough. But when it is slow, they nickel and dime the doctors for minor orders and sometimes even create drama between themselves or with the relatives of their patients."

But, as Nurse Kathy did with Ben, we need to occasionally ask: Is all the chaos experienced in these units intrinsic to the work setting? Or could some of that drama be created out of a need to feel connected?

If so, perhaps these nurses are unconsciously drawn into a field like intensive care because of the satisfaction they get from working in a chaotic environment. In other words, maybe they need/create chaos to experience the feeling of belonging. Freud would say they are drawn into this energy to revisit patterns from their childhood.

Dr. Dan's Drama

Dr. Dan was a busy obstetrician. He enjoyed his job and developed positive relationships with his co-workers and patients. However, his patients wondered why the delivery-room experience always was so chaotic; nurses running around, everyone yelling "PUSH" all the time. Several patients mentioned that their experiences in other deliveries weren't like that. Dr. Dan was like a different person in the delivery room. One patient noted that by the time the baby was delivered, Dr. Dan and his nurses were more exhausted than the mother and often screaming louder than the baby.

At a physician's workshop when discussing repetitive patterns, Dr. Dan had an epiphany. He said, "Now I get it. I grew up in a Jewish household with the stereotypical intrusive mother, the father that was never around, and three sisters that were classic Jewish-American princesses. We had unending drama in our home. A broken fingernail seemed to elicit the same response as a death in the family. Now I see that with all the female nurses running around the delivery room yelling, 'PUSH,' I feel perfectly at home with the drama."

Taking responsibility for the workplace dynamic places us in a unique and liberating position of power. Identifying the origin of the story and seeing how the past is brought into the present is similar to Freud's insights about repetition compulsions. The dysfunctional workplace is reminiscent of the dysfunctional family in many ways. The workplace becomes a place of acting out the unresolved pieces of our personal histories.

Dr. Dan realized that it wasn't the delivery that required this drama. He said that once he started to think about it, the word "push" never really needs to be used in a delivery room. He said it was probably quite obvious to a woman what to do. He wondered if he wasn't really just fulfilling some need he, and his staff, might have from past patterns.

Rose's story is another example.

Rose's Reflection

One evening, Rose, an emergency room nurse, was floated from the emergency room to the medical floor. Accustomed to the demands and intense drama of the ER, Rose found herself checking her patients every half hour. She checked vital signs, adjusted pillows, and reread charts. She spent the entire night bustling around. In the morning, one elderly patient noticed Rose in his room once more and asked,

36

"Nurse, am I really that sick?" Rose paused, looked at the patient, and replied, "No, I am."

Rose needed to feel busy and involved in order to feel like she was fulfilling her role as a healer. When she could not feel the energy of the fast-paced emergency room, she re-created the dynamic by hovering around her patients all night. In turn, a patient sensed the energy that Rose exuded and became worried that his condition was much worse that it really was. Where did that type of functioning come from? Did the patient need this chaos, or did Rose?

When Rose was a young girl, she had to give her diabetic mother insulin injections twice a day. Rose's mother was quite irresponsible with her medical management and so, after several physician visits, Rose decided to take over checking her blood-sugar levels and giving her insulin. Rose felt needed because of her mother's disease and because the doctors praised her when her mother's blood-sugar levels stabilized due to Rose's attentiveness.

After years of working in the same hospital, on the same floor, or in the same office, co-workers know each other like family; often like dysfunctional families.

Following is another example of how past energies can affect this workplace environment.

The Ties That Blind

Dr. Brown was raised in a strict military family. His father was a disciplinarian who demanded that the children follow rules and stay within tight boundaries. Most of Dr. Brown's interactions with his father involved some form of discipline. Later, as a physician, Dr. Brown found himself frequently being disciplined at work for inappropriate interactions. After a particularly tense meeting with the directing physician and another series of reprimands, he found himself again asking, "Why are they always picking on me?" He felt like everyone at work was against him. That night, he began to think about all of the unpleasant meetings he had endured with his director.

Suddenly, a realization emerged from his self-pity. Dr. Brown discovered that his behavior followed a clear, repetitive pattern. Whenever he didn't feel appreciated or acknowledged at work, he created a conflict that usually led to disciplinary action from his director. He realized he was unconsciously re-creating the father/son dynamic of his childhood because strict boundaries and discipline gave him a familiar sense of belonging.

Although Dr. Brown was not raised in an alcoholic home, his upbringing still made a powerful impact on his behavior. At first, Dr. Brown felt like his directing physician was intentionally pushing his buttons. He felt he was personally targeted by the director when, actually, Dr. Brown was investing his directing physician with qualities that turned him into a father/authority figure. This allowed him to continue playing an unconscious role that was familiar. Once he recognized this, he had the power to change his unconscious behavior patterns.

Revealing Patterns

Let's dig a little deeper by paying close attention to how we move, consciously or unconsciously, through our workdays. Because healthcare is a narrative field, the unhealed patterns that bind us are often revealed through the stories we tell. We create relationships with our co-workers and patients by telling stories. No one in healthcare needs to read romance novels or watch soap operas—it's the material of our day. We even tell stories to ourselves as our own inner dialogue arranges and narrates the events of the workday.

These stories can tell us a lot about who we are, what we value, and why we behave as we do. We may think that we are just talking, but often we are repeating ourselves ad nauseum because we are stuck in a psychological holding pattern. Our computer is endlessly printing the same page. We will keep telling the same tired story until we do the human homework necessary to release ourselves from the pattern.

It is said that when creative and spiritual energies are unused, they are expressed in less constructive and more destructive ways. Interpersonal tension, gossip, and negative blaming patterns keep us from maximizing our full collective potential at the workplace.

Finding our patterns and making them conscious builds our awareness muscle. This becomes challenging because when we unconsciously use drama, negativity, or neediness from our past to deal with people in the present, we are often left with the same depletion we experienced in childhood. As outlined in Freud's theory, situations *repeated* themselves so that Rose and Dr. Brown could eventually *remember* why they behaved the way they did.

The following is an exercise to help you see some of your patterns.

Exercise: *Finding Your Pattern First*

This exercise is designed to expose some of the unrecognized and unhealed wounds that contribute to the workplace dynamic.

First:
- Choose a story that you repeatedly tell about work or someone you work with.
- Listen to yourself tell the story or write it out in your journal.
- Identify which parts of the story trigger your emotions (e.g., the doctor makes you feel scared, the conflict makes you feel victimized, or the resolution makes you feel vindicated).

Next:
- Choose a story that you repeatedly tell about your childhood or upbringing.
- Listen to yourself tell the story or write it out in your journal. Identify the characters and emotions that are similar to the story you repeatedly tell about work. For example, do they both involve an authority figure, a mother/father figure, or a patient? Do you feel victimized?

Finally:
- Trace both stories to their origin. What took place in the past? How does it recur in the present? Does this pattern prevent the formation of good relationships with patients and/or co-workers? What can be done to stop deriving a sense of self from that story? What's the energetic drain here?

We are often completely unaware that we play out our own desires and needs through our stories. Participating in these patterns often leaves us feeling empty, fatigued, and burned out as we waste our energy. We prevent ourselves from being fully present to heal others and ourselves.

How do unhealed wounds hurt our patients and co-workers? Exploring this question will help us see how we contribute to the dynamic we experience in the workplace. Remembering Freud's Theory of repetition compulsion will help us to begin the process of stopping our patterned reactions. This is not just a superficial abstraction, but something potentially deeply transformative. With a little deeper probing, we find that our relationship to others is a direct extension of our relationship to ourselves. In fact, attunement to others first requires an attunement to self.

Rose, Dr. Brown, and Dr. Dan continually collided into unhealed pieces of themselves when they faced situations reminiscent of their childhood experiences. If we observe ourselves closely, we realize that we are repeating old patterns. But we can develop new qualities and ways of relating. And beyond the gift of locating the origin of our personal behavior patterns, we develop a greater awareness and understanding of the recurrent patterns manifested by our co-workers and patients.

Learning to recognize rote behavior patterns, taking responsibility for our workplace dynamic, and the healing process take time and practice. However, even the first steps in the healing process bring immediate benefits. Even just beginning to think of our workplace as having the potential to reveal our patterns creates a new context for healing ourselves as we heal others. This awareness begins to link our inner life and our healing with expanding our opportunities to practice better medicine.

This new awareness changes us. Soon, we find ourselves more energized at work and able to enjoy our work in a whole new way. We start to look forward to interacting with patients and co-workers, especially those who push our buttons. We begin to welcome the challenges that come our way. We are better prepared to meet the obstacles we face because we recognize their importance in our healing. But if we are to stop responding to our workplace in the same old ways, how *should* we respond?

What follows are seven ways to help awaken a more expansive psychological awareness. Developing such awareness will nurture you—what you do and how you do it.

Seven Techniques for Expanding Psychological Awareness

1. Learn to Manage Stress. Upon deeper introspection, realize that a co-worker or patient cannot make you angry or stressed out unless you allow them to. When someone throws up the middle finger at us at the freeway off-ramp, we react in anger. We seem to feel their finger triggered this response in us. But if the other driver made the same gesture and we had not seen it, would we have had the same response? Is it the gesture, or our awareness of the gesture that provokes us?

How do we hold this same type of awareness when working in a place guaranteed to traumatize all of us? On second thought, what better place, dense with emotion, is there for caretakers to learn what issues we bring into our interpersonal dynamics?

Between any stimulus and response, there is a space—a pause. When we are full of reactivity, we do not avail ourselves of that space. A choice lies within this space. Similar to the old "count to ten" technique, the meditative equivalent is to take a deep breath in and out through your nose. Breathing through the nose can act as a signal to the body's physiology that things are controllable, unlike mouth breathing that signals the fight-or-flight response. Instead of being the domino that falls when a chain reaction is set off, we can develop enough insight to change a reactive pattern. This perspective allows us to choose a response, instead of having a habitual reaction. Now, when a button gets pushed, we ask ourselves: What is the quality of my awareness here? Some learn through conscious use of breath that our tensions, given enough space, can actually be transformed into fuel. We can use this fuel to learn new ways to grow.

At first this probably cannot be done in the heat of the moment. It takes practice. Initially, it might take a week to ask this question and discern a response. But as we get more adept, the turnaround time decreases. All of our reactions, behaviors, thoughts, and feelings can serve the purpose of deepening our awareness, as can all of the places where we feel stuck, blocked, or brought to a standstill. These things now become a wake-up call to a deeper awareness of our true nature—signposts along our spiritual evolution. Instead of avoidance, we respond by looking within; exploring the areas where we need to be stretched and healed.

2. Lay Blame Aside. Blame and guilt are adaptive responses to situations where we feel overwhelmed and want to keep control. Both are a form of staying in control when a situation may be temporarily incomprehensible. To avoid blaming others and feeling victimized, we must find a way to stabilize a higher consciousness and pull ourselves and others up to that plateau. As long as we allow ourselves to blame others, we externalize the energy that could be better used for our own inner inquiry.

The next time you have a relationship conflict, resist the impulse to blame, defend, be right, or externalize your energies in any way. Instead, let the emotions surface and inquire about what is below them. Look for your deepest fear regarding the situation. Often you find a sense of inadequacy, inferiority, or intimidation has arisen. Seeing this, your unconscious patterns can be brought to your awareness. The old, automatic response of seeing someone else as the problem causing this emotion is replaced with a new reflex of inquiry into the energy aroused in you. The simple shift from blame to a new context will augment your receptivity and open you up for positive change.

3. Limit Yourself to Telling a Story Three Times. Previously we discussed looking for our patterning in the recurrent stories that we tell. Now we will look at how to use those stories. The energy drain from what we refer to as "bonding through bitching" is astronomical. Often, a complaint develops and people dwell on the story for weeks, months, or even years. Usually we are completely unaware of how distorted our memory is, and frequently our friends have heard our version of a story so many times they believe it to be fact even if it is only opinion.

If you are at a point where you want to reinforce a higher level of consciousness, try this technique: Limit the number of times you allow yourself to retell any experience. After telling a story three times, it becomes an entirely subjective tale that is only told from your point of view. Often, because memory is highly selective, the story does not even closely resemble what really happened.

Once you master limiting telling a story to no more than three times, try one of Gandhi's techniques of nonviolent communication. Try to tell the story one more time, telling exactly what happened without embellishing any details or supplementing it with emotions or perceptions. This leaves more energy inside you for assessing your part of the story instead of playing the blame game.

4. Track Your Energy. Becoming conscious of what gives us energy is important in our healing. What types of things excite you? What makes you miss lunch? What makes you go to a seminar? Would you sign up for that same conference if they did not offer Continuing Education Units?

Or, on another level, what drains your energy? Which co-workers get to you? What doctors get to you? What nurses get to you? Or even what patients annoy you? Have you ever noticed that the same people and patients do not bother everyone? What cases do you still talk about years after they have left your care? What are you really strongly attached to?

To learn about your personal energy, you have to begin to notice what motivates you, what puts you to sleep, and what gets you to a presentation. Is it the lunch offered, the brownie points with the boss, or is the topic of interest to you? This gives you a window of awareness into your personal dynamics. Once you have a different level of awareness, you have a different ability to make choices. Then, the next time we face a choice, we have more of ourselves to make that choice with. We have a better idea of who and what we are, and have greater trust in our ability to be honest with ourselves and to engage in what truly nourishes us. Then we can begin to care for ourselves and contribute to our own healing, which will directly affect our caring for others.

It is invigorating to find out where we are losing energy, and once we stop these recurrent leaks, we can save energy, invest it elsewhere, and even compound it as we become more present to those things along our path that stimulate our growth.

5. Practice Not Knowing. Most of us are fairly attached to the gifts of education. But after spending years in school, we may still feel incompetent. With all there is to know in medicine, we all need to learn to hold our knowledge in very humble containers. Getting comfortable in this humility, this inability to know everything, can be particularly hard for those in an education-intensive profession like medicine.

We spend a lot of time in healthcare focused on our education, training, and things that correlate with our intellectual quotient (IQ). Occasionally, we are fortunate enough that, despite our schooling, our interpersonal and our emotional quotient (EQ) has somehow remained intact. But for most of us, our spiritual quotient (SQ), or spiritual intelligence, has not gotten the nurturance and attention it needs to keep growing.

This humble not-knowing perspective is a very vulnerable yet refreshing place. A place that helps our SQ deepen. We are not talking about being proud of not knowing something we need to help a patient. We mean keeping a healthy spaciousness in our lives for the unexplained mysteries all around us. Certainly nothing is as common as birth and death—it happens to all of us and yet nothing is more miraculous, nothing comes with more unknowns or uncertainties. We may well understand the physical elements in birth, but past the physical-based reality, what are the emotional, spiritual, and more consciousness-based aspects that permeate this experience? These same questions and mysteries also surround death and dying. We are just beginning this inquiry.

Staying in a space of not knowing can enliven our day with mystery so that it does not become an empty ritual full of generic interactions and statistics. There is charm in the Zen beginner's mind—when we know what we lose when we think we know it all. It is refreshing to occasionally enter a situation from a place of not knowing and be secure with that. It allows us to open up into something deeper than our current understanding. Cultivating the place of not knowing gives us the freedom of an open and flexible mind. When we live with a sense of mystery, we are in a place where we are more willing and able to listen and learn from life's experiences.

6. Strengthen Weak Relationships. Often it is tempting to think of how nice it would be to work with functional people where everyone is perfect, but then reality intrudes. Accepting what is, and working from that, is a far better place to begin. Identify the co-worker that you have the poorest relationship with and meditate on both yourself and the energy you give off when you are around him or her. We hear our colleagues say things like, "Alan calls in sick so often that when I get invited to his funeral I'm going to think he's faking it." Or, "I wish Alan would just get here on time instead of making excuses about why he's so late. I'm to the point where I wouldn't care if his house burned down."

Find simple, subtle ways to be completely honest about this energy and stay in a meditative awareness. Do not allow an unbalanced focus to overtake you. This self-listening develops a certain level of presence that you can use with this person. Instead of thinking of what you are going to say in response to him or her, listen to that other person from a different energetic space. Take in what he or she says. Stop looking at a computer screen or have your nose in a chart while communicating with him. Notice his tone of voice, body language, vocabulary, and thus, the real meaning of what is being said. In this way, your response is much more likely to be coming from the current situation than from some past patterning.

7. Use Relationships as the Healers. If you place your relationships with your patients and co-workers in the context of them as your healers, you are then set up for a different pattern of relating altogether. Many psychology texts try to get us to see relationships as mirrors. Looking at relationships that way can help us to see parts of ourselves and can reveal our hidden patterns. Once you do see relationships as mirrors, you find there is no way to be in a relationship without being shaped by it.

From this perspective, every problem and every tension can push us further into self-inquiry. When people trigger in us a deep-seated emotional pattern, we often find that our reaction to the situation is out of proportion to the circumstances. This is a clue that we have bumped into an unhealed part of ourselves; that this is one of our reactive patterns. When relationships are viewed in this manner, we find ourselves actually seeking something or someone who really bugs us at work, because now that can be changed into a very helpful method to further our conscious evolution. This brings an opportunity to turn our emotion inward and use this interaction for our own healing.

For example, frequently loaded interactions between a nurse and a physician or between a doctor and the hospital CEO are not just about the two people, but about how we interact with authority figures. Once we see this, we have the opportunity to grow. Freud reminds us that although we can avoid this awareness, the same situations will keep arising until we are ready to get the lesson of the encounter. When we allow our relationships to teach, we can begin to heal some of the wounds that become evident in our workplace.

Integrate these seven techniques into your workday and you will find yourself gradually developing a new awareness.

Healing Awareness
What a great gift it would be if we could create an environment, both internally and externally, for ourselves that nurtures our emotional and psychological healing. In order for our patients, Mr. Smith, Mrs. Frederick, and Mr. Peters

from the beginning of the chapter, to really heal, they will need more than good medical care. They will need to take control of their thoughts and break the *remember/repeat* cycle. They need to develop spaciousness for self-observation. Then, as they learn to process their behaviors, they will discover a healthy awareness that will replace the false sense of well-being they gleaned from negative patterns. Instead of feeling disheartened, they can use their current situation as a departure point from which they will begin to create a more meaningful dynamic for themselves. So too with us. We need to discover a new awareness in our workplace relationships instead of holding on to our addictions such as blaming, drama, and the need to be right.

Personal development means to grow as human beings, to engage in reflection and activities that put us in touch with the deeper core of our humanity. It means to find some space to get out of the noise and rush of daily life, to feel for at least a few moments each day, the reality of our inner lives, our deeper shared humanity. You chose to be a healthcare worker. Now you can you choose your attitude in that profession as well. Unhealed healers who do not grow and cultivate this deep part of themselves will remain ungrounded in their own vocation.

In the next chapter, we will continue to learn how to increase our spiritual awareness as a way of expanding our healing. We will look into some fundamental spiritual tenets that will empower us to take control of our patterns. The antidote for a lot of what has been lost to us personally is a renewed sense of spirituality.

Chapter 5
Practicing Self-Reflection

"Do not be conformed to this world, but be transformed by the renewing of your mind."
—Romans 12:1–2

Our workplace is an endless source of challenges. Most of us are well-trained to meet the scientific challenges of our jobs but poorly trained when it comes to recognizing the spiritual possibilities in our work. Healthcare's spiritual foundation has been overlooked. How can we use spirituality as a stimulus for expanding our development, both personally and professionally?

This chapter will focus on recrafting some ancient spiritual principles, untethering them from their religious traditions and reappropriating them for our use. There's no intent here to try to change or influence anyone's religious or spiritual beliefs. Instead, we seek to reveal ideas that pertain to universal spirituality rather than any one particular religion. By culling the spiritual concepts of synchronicity, karma, witnessing, meditation, self-inquiry, presence, awareness, letting go, gratitude, and compassion, we will try to bring a new spiritual framework to the ever-changing and stress-filled dynamics of our workplace. The aim is to create a smorgasbord of alternative ways to view our relationship with ourselves, our co-workers, our patients, and our workplaces.

Embracing these spiritual principles helps us deepen our awareness of the human condition. This awareness is a major factor in helping us evolve from a conceptual spirituality and a conceptual compassion to something more integrated in our workplace interactions. As we experiment with these concepts, we evolve our own spiritual wellness—a wellness that should be foundational in our field. It is unfortunate that medical education does not include the development of spiritual wellness as an essential element in its curriculum.

The reality is that spirituality is interwoven into our workplace interactions on a daily basis, whether we are conscious of it or not. Relationships fill our workplaces, and many spiritual traditions center their richest practices and deepest wisdom in the context of relationships.

Akin to Dorothy in *The Wizard of Oz*, we travel down the yellow brick road of spiritual discovery. As Dorothy progresses, she reowns parts of herself—her mind, her heart, and her courage. She faces an externalized power, the all-powerful wizard who sends her back to address her shadow. As she continues to discover parts of her authentic self, she returns to find Toto (nature/spirituality) uncovering a well-intended man behind a machine (technology) who is demonized by people's expectations of him. Sound familiar?

We can find this same journey as we walk the halls of our hospitals or healthcare settings. Our journey has all the same challenges, the same potential for a transformation in consciousness. Leaving our comfort zone is an essential first step in the classic hero's journey. Odysseus, for example, like Dorothy, had to leave his home to become a famous warrior. The moment we decide to change our patterns, we leave the familiar and begin our journey.

When we take responsibility for personal relationships in the workplace instead of viewing ourselves as victims, we may feel unsure of our path. But the seduction of our patterns can pull us off our course and leave us shipwrecked on the shores of our own unconscious patterns. So like Odysseus, to avoid being tricked by the Sirens, we will have to tie ourselves to some spiritual principles.

The First Step

Dr. Sanjo recognized that he treated all the nurses with the same distance and thinly veiled contempt that he felt for his domineering mother. Once he recognized this behavior, he decided he wanted to change the way he related to nurses. The next morning, he saw a nurse named Michelle walking toward him down the hallway. "What do I do? What do I say?" he asked himself.

In this situation, Dr. Sanjo is ready to embark on a hero's journey. He knows he needs to change his behavior, but he does not yet have the skills to communicate on a different level. We change from ordinary people into heroes by leaving the familiar and venturing out into the unknown. Dr. Sanjo needs to develop a spiritual toolbox that will allow him to release old habits so that he will be free to develop new behaviors. Spiritual growth begins when we want to move beyond being victims of patterned behavior. We must desire to change. We must make a conscious choice to change.

A Young Monk's Quest

A young monk was told by his teacher that getting to the top of a certain mountain was something that would bring enlightenment. He began his journey by hiking for many days through fields and forests. When he approached the foothills of the mountain, he found a wide river blocking his way. As a spiritual pilgrim, he pondered the significance of the river for several days. (Something spiritual pilgrims apparently do.) He decided that the river would not prevent him from reaching the top of the mountain. He returned to the forest, gathered some wood, and spent a lot of time crafting a strong and beautiful raft. Then he set out to cross the river. The raft carried him quickly and safely across.

The raft was so helpful that when he reached the opposite side he picked it up and began to carry it up the mountain with him. Soon, the raft became burdensome. His legs began to stumble and he stooped under the weight. He could no longer stand straight enough to survey the land, let alone continue to climb the tall mountain. Although he was grateful to the raft for carrying him across the river, he realized he would have to let go of the raft to reach his goal.

So when he came to a point where the raft did not serve him anymore, the monk gave it up. But it took some time to do this. Similarly, we need to let go of the patterns that block our personal growth. These rote-behavior patterns, like a raft on dry land, block us from achieving our goals. Once released, we generate the energy needed to develop in new directions.

The following are some spiritual tools that can be especially useful in the workplace for continuing this development: We will define the spiritual principle and then supply some background so that you can see the application of the spiritual teaching in the context of our workplace.

Eight Spiritual Principles for Developing Workplace Awareness

1. Spiritual Principle: Understand That Things Happen for a Reason

Spiritual Background: In Christianity's highest prayer is the phrase "Thy will be done." This is a deep form of trusting that things happen for a reason.

Hindus feel that relationships are life's way of using another person or situation to trigger something new in us. The Hindu concept of karma teaches that there is a purpose hidden within the seemingly random way people and situations come together.

Such meetings are called "divine appointments" in the Religious Science tradition. In this tradition, these seemingly random encounters occur in order to invite us into a greater awakening.

Recognizing the spiritual reason for why we end up in certain places with certain people requires a shift in the way we think. Like the Zen koan, "What is the sound of one hand clapping?" there is often no linear way to understand why certain things are presented to us. We learn by expanding our questioning about them and remaining open to an array of possible answers.

In the Buddhist tradition there is a practice that focuses on culling the understandings available in any situation. This practice is called, "Why me? Why this? Why now?" It is exactly that—asking these three questions of ourselves in any situation as a way of exploring the deeper meaning of an encounter.

Buddhists also feel that "when a student is ready, a teacher appears." This belief focuses us on each encounter as a teacher/guru, allowing us to see how a situation might be arising in order to point us toward a new understanding.

Adopting the perspective that "things happen for a reason" forces an inquiring mind to pause and look deeper into things. This pause can create spaciousness in our thinking—a spiritual way to keep us evolving.

Spiritual Application: Many of us can acknowledge the perspective that "things happen for a reason" in our personal lives, but we find it harder to bring that awareness into our workplace. When we get the demanding patient or end up working with a difficult supervisor, we tend to discard the spiritual logic of this perspective. But the next time you begin to judge a situation that you are in, consider: Did you, on some unknown level, attract this experience into your life? Are these events occurring to teach you a new awareness about a particular behavior? Is this situation brought to you for your own healing?

The Buddhist practice of "Why Me? Why This? Why Now?" can be particularly helpful here. This practice bypasses the contraction of judgment or blaming others and puts us directly in the center of the experience. In this practice, we become aware that events are not just happening *to* us, they are happening *for* us. (Even if this is not true, it can be a very helpful way to frame a situation.)

For example, anyone who takes night call knows that it is fairly easy to wake up at 4 AM with a rather toxic attitude. Integrating the awareness of "Why me? Why this? Why now?" can be another way of asking, "Why is this happening to me? What does this particular situation have to teach me, and why, for goodness sake, does it have to happen at 4 AM?"

Something Shifts

Dr. Clark lies down in the call room after a long, exhausting day. Just as his body begins to relax, and his eyes slowly shut, the phone rings. "Dr. Clark, STAT delivery in room four. It's a twenty-six weeker, maternal heroin use."

Dr. Clark, sleep deprived and hungry, is at the point when willpower succumbs to exhaustion. He inhales some junk food from the hospital vending machine on the way to the delivery. As he has done a hundred times before, he arrives irritable and disconnected from any deeper purpose he once may have found in his job. He no longer arrives to attend a birth, but focuses on how to get this delivery over with as quickly as possible so he can get back to bed. He silently wonders, "Why does this always happen to me?" Then he remembers the Buddhist method of inquiry, "Why me? Why this? Why now?"

The questions still echoing in his head, he enters the delivery room. The young addict, though tired and frightened, nonetheless sincerely thanks him for coming. Dr. Clark's perspective begins to soften. A connection is made. Something invisible is touched. He realizes he is here because he may have something to learn. He begins to wonder what in this woman's life drove her to use heroin.

Dr. Clark is pulled into something more than being a detached participant in a delivery. As this three-question practice kicks in, he thinks, "Could this be happening to me for a reason? Why did this lady come in on my night call? Why at 4 AM? Could there be a reason for my being hungry and sleep deprived?" After the delivery, he continues to ponder these questions. The spiritual correlates begin to appear.

"Why the hunger?" he wonders. Fasting, he recalls, is something done in many spiritual traditions, including his own. He knows that fasting is believed to make people more receptive to prayer or meditation. "Why this sleep deprivation?" He remembers, back in high school, visiting an Italian monastery where the monks practiced sleep deprivation to make themselves more receptive to prayer and meditation. Similarly, Dr. Clark feels married night after night to his job in the way the monks describe being married to the church.

Gradually a new perspective emerges. His previous self-pitying questions, "Why me? Why this? Why now?" are transformed into a meditation on why he was in the delivery room at that moment. At the next delivery, the same questions asked in a different situation left Dr. Clark overwhelmingly grateful for the opportunity to awaken from a sleep more profound than the exhaustion he felt in the call room.

Few would question the intrinsically spiritual nature of our work. But Dr. Clark's story illustrates how easily this spiritual development can be overlooked when we are sleep deprived. Once we decide to have a more spiritual conversation with our work, we will find that there is no way of being in this dialogue without being formed by it. Using the material of our day, we no longer have to wait for a coincidence too powerful to ignore before we wake up to the lesson being presented.

2. Spiritual Principle: Be Present and Open

Spiritual Background: From the Hindu concept of the "I Don't Know Mind," to the Zen "Beginner's Mind," to the Catholic "Cloud of Unknowing," many faiths honor a mind-set that is empty and clear. A mind that does not cling to static beliefs or ideas. The Hindus have a saying that a river looks like the same river every day, yet there is not one drop of water that is the same. A Buddhist expression says that if a man has been married for ten years and his wife goes out of their house for ten minutes, on her return he is vain to think he knows her. Allowing a space of openness and "not knowing," then we begin to develop a humility of knowing, which is an act of generosity.

Spiritual Application: Back to our example of Dr. Sanjo and his not knowing how to relate to the nurse. What should he say? How should he respond to her? Believe it or not, the easiest way to change a thought process is to stop thinking. Instead of worrying about what and how, Dr. Sanjo can learn to be open to whatever Michelle may say or do. Can he find a quality of presence that allows him to be nonjudgmental and motiveless when listening or simply being with another? When we show up in a context with our full presence, we learn in both the ordinary and extraordinary interactions in our workday.

The ability to be fully present in any given moment means abandoning what we think we know and allowing knowledge to reveal itself moment by moment. Asking "What do I not know here?" allows us to reside in an attitude of receptivity. Of course, this is not a very functional way of being if a patient is coding, so we have to be somewhat discriminatory when using these principles. That is why we are focusing our inquiry on relationships.

Reciprocity

Sonya had always dreamed of having children. When she had her first child, she took a leave of absence from her career so she could be a stay-at-home mom. She felt very comfortable with her baby's needs such as feeding, diapering, and soothing, but what she did not expect was the fact that all these needs were so time intensive. The tasks left her little time to tackle anything else on her never-ending to-do list. At first, she was distraught and even frustrated with herself because she was used to getting so much done in a day and being efficient.

But as time went on, what she learned from her child was the ability to be in the moment—the present. Children operate in the moment and often we adults find ourselves in the past or concerned about the next thing that has to happen—the future. Sonya realized that her child was actually teaching her to be in the moment and let go. She loved her child, as any parent does, with the rawness of her being, yet she never expected a gift such as this. She savored the moments as they came and realized one of the many reciprocities of parenting

3. Spiritual Principle: Meditate

Spiritual Background: Buddhists feel that medicine is an ideal way to explore spirituality. Medicine is felt to be meditation in action. In fact, the words meditation and medicine come from the same root. Medicine means that which heals the physical, and meditation means that which heals the spiritual.

In the Tibetan tradition, a physician's ability to be a deep healer is directly proportional to the degree of his or her spiritual awakening. Meditation develops our capacity to be present.

Buddhists have an expression: "Nothing is so fragile as action without meditation." Meditation is more of a state, or a context, than an activity. That state is easier to maintain in a Himalayan cave or on a cushion with closed eyes. It is easy to idealize the Buddha and his meditative presence. The typical garden sculpture of Buddha is always serene, smiling, rain or shine, despite bird droppings or bodily needs. But we are not statues. We need a vision that is more integrated into the reality of our daily lives. It becomes more complicated with eyes open and even more challenging when it involves feelings and interactions with others. Many Buddhists use breath as the object of meditation, but using patients, co-workers, and even oneself is possible, though more difficult. Medicine can be viewed as a spiritual practice, a social meditation of synchronicity.

One of meditation's greatest gifts is that it can turn us into our own psychotherapists. Our mind can learn to objectively reflect on itself, so we can be more present in any moment. This presence comes not from suppressing thoughts, but from breaking our identification with them. A spaciousness is developed so that we can recognize the energy in which thoughts arise. This can be a very helpful when we are engrossed in intense physical and emotional experiences of our workdays.

A practicing meditator gradually receives the tangible gifts of a meditative awareness: a lack of a rush to speak, deeper listening, and a poise of heart that extinguishes haste. This state of meditative awareness becomes a reference point, a place inside us that our roles cannot touch. Instead we say and do things connected to this underlying state, whether touching others, listening to them, reaching out to them in some way, or just being with them in silence. Meditation transcends the whole level of ego where motivations dwell, putting the mind more in touch with the deeper levels of values that underlie motivations. Like those Buddha statues in our gardens, we smile from a deep contentment when our life has the flavor of this meditative awareness. Meditation is a way of training or developing the posture of a witness in your interactions.

Spiritual Application: Transporting meditation and mindfulness from the monastery into the daily workplace can take many forms. In America most of us are usually about one stoplight away from being late for work. How then do we find time in our harried lives to insert the richness of meditation? Perhaps in unexpected ways.

In one hospital, for instance, cameras were placed in the delivery rooms to film the resuscitation of infants so that residents, fellows, and nursing students could witness and discuss their interventions. This is a form of witnessing, of meditation. To witness is to openly observe and respond rather than react in a knee-jerk fashion. Over the years in this hospital, an impressive diminution has occurred in the drama and activity in the delivery room. Observation has infused a calmer, more peaceful presence. In the Buddhist meditative tradition, it was not unusual for beginning meditators to spend extended periods of time meditating on the bodies of corpses before cremation, sitting with the emotions that arise when confronted with the stark reality of death.

4. Spiritual Principle: Employ Near-Enemy Practice

Spiritual Background: The Christian tradition teaches us to love our enemy.

In many spiritual traditions, enemies are felt to be the major provocateurs of spiritual advancement. The Buddhist Near-Enemy Practice starts with the premise that as long as people are interacting meaningfully, conflicts will exist. This practice teaches us to take the biggest enemy or difficulty we have at work, whether it is a co-worker, patient, or situation, and turn that into our teacher. In Hinduism, these difficult people are said to be the assassins we hire unknowingly to disassemble our egos.

Spiritual Application: Think about the most difficult person at work. It may be a colleague, a boss, or even a patient or his or her family member. With our current thinking, it may be a stumbling block in your day or something that you dread as you enter your workplace. With this new perspective we learn that adversaries are needed in order to develop and refine our interpersonal skills. These so-called adversaries, or difficult people, may actually point us toward our limitations and, in turn, shed light on an area for our growth.

Instead of avoiding those who push our buttons, we must ask ourselves to dive into situations and plunge into the feelings they arouse. We must allow our irritations to be our teachers. Just as an irritant of sand can create a pearl, these irritant teachers and the emotions they bring up push us deeper and deeper into the questions that fuel the pearl of spiritual deepening. We can ask ourselves: "Why is this situation repeating itself over and over again? What am I to learn from it? How can I make friends with it and move beyond it?"

5. Spiritual Principle: Practice Self-Inquiry

Spiritual Background: A continuous, ceaseless deepening of inquiry can bring a new richness to anything we do. The deepening of the question "Who am I?" is a form of inquiry used in many spiritual traditions. This particular question is a way of trying to get practitioners past the place where their sense of self is derived completely from their ego. For us it would be getting us to a place where our sense of self is not derived entirely from our role.

This form of questioning points us to an understanding of something deeper, something more innate than our role. This may be akin to what sometimes happens to hospice patients who, over time, shed layers and layers of their personality until deeper parts of their being are revealed as their former roles lose their meaning.

In order to know ourselves better, we will have to cultivate a poise of heart that creates receptivity to the situations at hand. For a healer to truly understand his or her vocation, he or she needs to be receptive to healing as a reciprocal energy exchange. An unhealed healer, a role-based performer, does not know how to truly participate in the fundamental meaning of healing. To transcend the role or current concept of healer, we only need to change one thing, begin to inquire into the belief that we are giving and not receiving.

Spiritual Application: Self-inquiry is a technique that teaches how to study our own personal experience. "Experience" is the Latin root for "experiment," and this technique of inquiry helps us experiment with our own experiences. In any given situation, we can ask ourselves, "Who am I in this situation? Why am I experiencing this right now? What am I being while I am experiencing this?" As we continue this type of inquiry, the goal is learning to subtract our sense of self from our experience. First, we learn not to take things personally. Then something which transcends the personal takes over and we can then relate to anything from a state of peace where the personal agenda is out of the way.

Dr. Lee's Personal Reflection

Dr. Lee had been doing anesthesia for years. Becoming more conscious of the ebb and flow of energy in his day, he began to notice his stress level when intubating a patient. He realized over time that when he went to intubate a patient, he did not breathe from the time he started until he finished, and this always stressed him to hurry. He then learned in a retreat that fixity of attention is enhanced by slowness of breath. When breathing through one's nose, slowly and consciously, something is activated, a slowing-down response, that does not come with stressful mouth breathing.

Dr. Lee used his personal awareness to study his own experience. He found a problem and took it to a different level of inquiry that helped him transcend an area where he felt stuck. He did this without support from anyone. No outside funding required. He felt richly reimbursed by the positive energy he added to his day.

As we deepen our inquiry, we uncover the link between self-inquiry and collective inquiry. One of the privileges of being in such a rich profession is that as we grow, the profession seems to expand and develop right along with us. Our experience of our profession changes as we change.

Suzie's New Position

Suzie left her job as a pediatric intensive care nurse for several years in order to raise a family. After a few years, her husband was laid off and Susie had to return to work. She really was not that interested in returning to something she had done for over a decade. She was turned off by all she had heard about the current state of nursing and how it had become so much more task oriented.

But when she got to her job, she found that she too had changed. She was delighted to find that the charting and administrative issues that bothered most nurses did not affect her. She told people that the job had not changed, but she had.

She came back with a different quality of presence, now knowing the pain and love of parenting, which enhanced her pediatric nursing more than any conference she had ever attended.

6. Spiritual Principle: Know Yourself

Spiritual Background: Islam teaches that if a person knows himself or herself, they know God. "Know thyself" are the words at the entrance to the Oracle of Delphi, but knowing oneself is only half the story. Having the courage to *be* one's self is the other half. It is said that Buddha's last words were "Be a light unto yourself." In the Christian gospels, Paul exhorts, "Do not model yourselves on the behavior of the world around you, but let your behavior be modeled by your new mind."

Spiritual Application: When we begin to know ourselves, we begin to understand how we relate to our co-workers, family and friends, and the universe around us. While we want to avoid falling into the mind-set that we know ourselves so well that we can predict how we will react to certain people and situations, it is important to know what types of events will trigger positive as well as negative reactions. This then allows us to bring in an inner self-awareness to all we do. Our quest is to integrate this self-knowledge into our experience.

Sarah

Sarah was at a lecture, listening to a doctor whom she had worked with years ago. She was amazed to find him speaking about nursing in such a positive light. She had always had the impression that he did not really like or respect nurses. After the lecture, she went up to tell him this, only to find to her surprise that as she started talking, her awareness blossomed. She mentioned thinking that he did not like nurses, and then she thought how actually most of the doctors she interacted with she felt the same about. On further reflection, she realized she felt the same about many of the administrators.

Slowly, it came out in their conversation that she seemed to project a lot of distrust and dislike on any authority figure in her life. When asked where that dynamic may have come from, she said she had been raised in a series of foster families, always being persona non grata, never sure when she would be moved to the next home. This dynamic of fear caused a generalized problem with all authority—projecting her fear onto them and dreading the consequences.

7. Spiritual Principle: Develop Compassion

Spiritual Background: In Buddhism, God is said to be the personification of a person's most compassionate self. Buddhists also believe compassion is the seed of enlightenment. The two-thousand-year-old Buddhist vow, the Bodhisattva vow, is very similar to medicine's Hippocratic Oath. It is a commitment that allows for the development of our own enlightenment by deeply connecting with, and serving, others.

Compassion is at the core of healing. Sometimes just being a compassionate witness to another's pain, experiencing the raw reality of suffering, pulls us down from higher spiritual altitudes into the human experience. This can be humbling as well as healing. When faced with an individual in pain, our instincts and training tell us to distance ourselves. By distancing ourselves from pain, we distance ourselves from one another and lose the grounding of our shared humanity—the very connection that makes compassion possible.

In Buddhism, there are Four Noble Truths, the first paraphrased as, "You are going to suffer." Buddhism helps us understand that it is only through our suffering that we find strength, compassion, and our need to connect with others. We gain insights into ourselves and into a transpersonal realm of spiritual experiences with others.

The Christian tradition has many examples of how everything that suffers (or burns out, as we have termed the experience) is up for the possibility of resurrection. Resurrection is an archetypal image illustrating how we can be resuscitated from our disconnection to life.

Spiritual Application: Medical and nursing schools teach various techniques for interviewing, collecting data, and examining a patient, but very little about compassion. Shouldn't we be spending as much time on developing compassion as learning computer skills? Somehow, we have lost the sense that spirituality is hard work and requires a lot of discipline. Our scientific training has overpowered our ability to hear the secret whispering of our hearts, which tells us that our jobs are intimately entwined with spirituality.

Dr. Sanjo Returns

When Dr. Sanjo stops in the hallway to talk with Nurse Michelle, he recognizes that she sometimes reminds him of his domineering mother because she is not afraid to call his mistakes to his attention, but he decides to be present and open to what she says. After a brief good morning, Nurse Michelle tells Dr. Sanjo that he failed to get a required consent completed. Instead of reacting out of indignant efficiency, Dr. Sanjo listens with compassion. He realizes that he created extra work and chaos for her by forgetting to sign the paperwork. He apologizes to her. In turn, Nurse Michelle thanks him for being a respectful listener and for understanding her point of view and rectifying the situation. Through compassion, Dr. Sanjo overcame a patterned reaction and turned a potentially negative experience into a positive encounter.

For us, as with Dr. Sanjo, compassion is a quality that can be developed. By distancing ourselves from pain, we distance ourselves from one another and lose the grounding of our shared humanity—the connection that makes compassion possible. Compassion is not just *knowing* the feelings of others, but *feeling* their feelings. To do this work, we first have to know the feelings of our own woundings. In the words of Henri Nouwen, author of *The Wounded Healer*, "Making one's own wounds a source of healing requires the constant willingness to see one's own pain and suffering as rising from the depth of the human condition which all people share."

Compassion is the courageous expression of sincere love and understanding for the people around us. It is an active feeling, a desire to share in another person's burden and/or accompany them on their joyous journey. We may find it easy to feel compassion toward patients, especially when their suffering is acute. It may be more difficult to be compassionate toward our co-workers, but both situations offer us an opportunity reach to another in loving kindness that leads to mutual healing.

One of the greatest spiritual gifts of medicine is that our workday provides us daily opportunities for compassionate giving when we are mindful enough to realize it.

8. Spiritual Principle: Accept What Is

Spiritual Background: In some forms of Buddhism, the ultimate meditation is said to be simply accepting what is, not thinking about what was or what should be. When we accept things as they are, we get to see something greater than we can see when we are expecting something to change. Real meditation is a state of pure welcoming—there is no choosing of whatever appears in the field of consciousness. Everything is allowed equally because the mind has ceased trying to manipulate our experience.

Sometimes, accepting that what is happening is the right thing to be happening can give us a perspective that can be very instructive. When we can remain internally aligned with whatever form a moment takes, a richness can appear that is otherwise invisible.

Spiritual Application:

On the Spiritual Path

Nurse Terry made an interesting observation. She mentioned that she would occasionally come into work and not want her patient assignment—be it a sick baby with a cardiac lesion, or a child with some extremely high-maintenance parents. With her current seniority, she would occasionally change her assignment to an easier patient. Over time, she noticed that when she did this, the patient she avoided seemed to have a stable day or the parents did not require as much support, and the easier patient she rearranged to get often ended up in some crisis.

Eventually, Terry began to think that she might be better off not trying to rearrange her assignments. Instead, she tried to stay present for whatever lesson life might be bringing her. As a result, she is now changed her perspective and has a deeper appreciation for whatever shows up. Instead of changing what seemed an unsatisfactory situation, she seeks to change herself, to look deeper and make her day a practice in opening to what is. Now she tries not to miss what lesson might be concealed in whatever form her day takes, knowing this might be life's way of nudging her growth.

Years later, Terry has developed a clear depth of understanding for the lesson that is being presented in any situation. It is possible to almost hear her inner spaciousness arising as she says, "Hmmm ... interesting," knowing she is as interested in herself being in this situation as in the situation itself.

When we allow reality to be our guru, we find that with some of our patients, knowledge is power, and for others, ignorance is bliss. If we can accept their preference, we can learn to be smart with smart people and simple with simple ones. Many healthcare workers tend to become set in just one model of personal relationships. But, really, our task is to learn to relate to many people in many different ways. Such options enable us to exercise an expansiveness with our patients and within ourselves.

Applied Spirituality

If we invite spirituality into our workplace, we recognize that there is more to healing than just skills and training. Using the above spiritual principles are a few examples of ways to transform our workplace encounters by grounding them in and applied spirituality. In this ancient practice of spiritual development, Bodhisattvas (seekers of enlightenment) have found a systematic method to apply spiritual principles to their own path of deepening. The essence of Buddhist spirituality, it seems, is to tend to the physical and emotional illness of others. In this tradition, monks start with healing their personal wounds, move on to access their creativity, and then progress to enlightenment based on serving others. From this perspective, a Bodhisattva is exposed to lessons so profound that they transcend interpersonal connection to a more universal transformation.

When we decide to change our outlook and environment, we need to remember that we are undertaking a journey. We may stumble at first. Situations may catch us off guard, and we may find that we resort to old behavior patterns instead of using a new tool from our spiritual toolbox. But in the end, the fabric of our day begins to become the source of our own spiritual deepening, and this refreshed focus brings out in us a more creative, loving, and open way, of interacting with others.

Chapter 6
Refreshing the Healer/Patient Connection

"I slept and dreamed that life was joy. I awoke and saw that life was service acted and behold, service was joy."
—Rabindranath

Our job, when performed with a developed spiritual focus, places us in the midst of our shared humanity with our patients. It calls upon us to be a witness to their experience and to share their suffering in a spiritual way. To fully expand and express our spirituality at the workplace, we must awaken the godhead that lies within that witnessing connection.

In this chapter, we will look at how healing connects us to our patients. Our goal is to create a context in our workplace in which the series of continual relationships we encounter can provide a nourishing psychic soil for our growth. No plant does well in a pot too small to allow its growth. Similarly, if we restrict our understanding to the current medical culture, we will find ourselves confined in a system that does not always encourage our full expansion.

In previous chapters, we discussed the core archetype of a healer, something intrinsic to most of us who have chosen the healing arts as our profession. This core, the force in the center of our soul that keeps us engaged and generative, is something we need to nurture and respect. How do we become better witnesses for the experience of our patients? How do we restore a sense of sacredness to a medical world distracted by technological complexities?

Paying Homage
First, we must pay homage to what originally drew us to the healing arts. This is the part of us we want to reclaim, heal, and nurture. When we lose touch

with what motivated us to enter medicine, we often end up unconsciously trapped in the confines of a role that does not permit us to truly connect with the emotional experience of our patients or ourselves.

Few of us came into this field because of our fascination with technology or our ability to execute precise tasks with complete perfection. If so, we might as well have become tattoo artists or accountants. The question is, how do we work in tandem with technology so that it does not violate our human need for deeper connections?

There is a distinction between curing a disease and healing the patient. Healing means returning someone to their wholeness. We can often cure a body with our science, but to truly heal requires a commitment that runs deeper than technology and machinery.

If we commit to healing, we end up with an expanded psychological and spiritual context for our work. That change also directs us toward a deeper understanding of how we heal. On the most basic level, the holistic movement made us aware of the distinction between suppressing symptoms and healing. This perspective led to a change in view. We now seek not just recovery from a disease or symptom, but removal of the underlying cause of a physical or psychological condition. An even larger understanding of healing has developed from this expanded awareness.

Without understanding the larger picture of healing, there are no healers. Instead, we end up as human mechanics focused only on the body part in question. To activate this evolving awareness in our workplace, we need to look beyond our technological focus and the arrogance of science, to something outside our current understanding.

What if we evolved and developed a paradigm with a mutual healing potential between the patient and healer? The healer helps the patient by using psychological and spiritual resources as well as science. Simultaneously, the patient could stimulate healing within the healer by encouraging the development of wholeness that happens within the spiritual connection between humans. Instead of maintaining the classic professional relationship, which often means one of distance, we should encourage a compassionate reciprocal relationship, where the healer and the patient are healing each other. We have all had a few patients who have pulled us to this level of understanding. This completely transforms the healer/patient relationship, equalizing the energy and spawning many changes in our interactions.

In order to have this type of transformative relationship on a more consistent basis, we must revitalize the static construct of the healer/patient relationship and bring in a new context where roles can be redefined, and even reversed in certain situations. If you think for a moment about one or two patients who touched you most, you will most likely find these are patients who somehow drew you out of your role into a different type of relationship. Something about those patients left a unique impression. You may remember something specific about them: a thought they shared at a vulnerable time, some way they permitted you to access new parts of yourself in conversation, a heightened sense of compassion, or their gratitude when they might have complained. You may not even be conscious of why they touched you. Some patients just have the ability to tug us out of the robotic, inert nature of the workday mind-set and bring us back to the essence of healing. Throughout this chapter, keep in mind the healing encounters that have given you this deeper connection. By studying those special relationships, we can consciously pursue that sort of connection or awareness in every patient encounter.

Of course, most patients come in for physical healing. But if we redirect our thinking to a deeper level, we can imagine that they come in for psychological and spiritual healing as well. Deeper yet, if you add the caregiver into the mix, both the patient as well as the caregiver may be seeking healing, even if on different levels. One may be seeking physical healing; the other may be seeking psychological or spiritual healing. We have the chance to have encounters where both the patient and the caregiver experience mutual healing, instead of one being cured and the other drained. What are our current barriers to accessing this mutual healing? They begin with the simple lack of the awareness of this potential.

From Communication to Communion

As in any relationship, the quality of communication largely determines its potential. To expand the potential of the healing duo, we must improve the communication. In many situations, we use technical jargon while trying simultaneously to translate information into layman's terms. By hiding behind the technical language, we separate ourselves from our patient and lose any opportunity to receive the gifts of the encounter. This often demonstrates how we are acting in our role-based behaviors instead of with deep intent to connect reciprocally.

Communication Yields Ultimate Connection

Baby Aaron was on ECMO (heart-lung bypass) and had a heart defect, overwhelming sepsis, and Down syndrome. There were many conversations, consults, and opinions about the course of care. Wanting to be very involved, the parents maintained a vigil at the bedside constantly.

Seeing the many physicians and nurses at Aaron's bedside, the parents assumed their baby was progressing. But, finally given statistics on

Aaron's medical situation, they hung their heads in despair. Clearly, they had misread the hustle and bustle of the medical professionals. The parents inferred that the busyness of the professionals around the bedside, and the use of medical jargon, meant that progress was being made.

But now that it was clear that their baby was not getting better, the issue became ways to make him more comfortable, given the inevitability of death.

Together with the social workers, the nurses, and the doctors, the mother and father were able to formulate a plan of care for Aaron. The communication became a sacred communion of compassionate souls. Healing happened, surrounded with the common human languages of silence, compassion, and love.

Using a role-based verbal shield creates a communication barrier, a separation between us and our patients. If we were to embrace a different type of communication, we might find our conversations to have a mutual richness that is greater than the current routine of downloading data to patients. The verbal disconnection we come across daily in our work, shows there are defective interactions on a much deeper level, more so than mere medical-speak.

A Participatory Reality
When we begin our engagement by asking about a patient's feelings or understanding, we open up a participatory reality. This interaction not only gives insight into a patient's thinking, but it also shows them our receptivity. They may not be an expert in their disease, but everyone is an expert in their own feelings and can be engaged when this level, which bypasses intimidation, is opened up first. It does not take long to recognize that many patients are hurting in ways we can only begin to imagine. Instead of the rote, role-based encounters, this introduction realigns the ability to relate to one another on a deeper level.

The prayer of St. Francis of Assisi is a step-by-step method for deepening interpersonal connection. One line can be paraphrased as, "God grant that I may never seek more to be understood than to understand." We cannot underestimate the importance this shift in perspective gives in nearly every encounter. Think about approaching another with the intent to understand them before downloading your data. How can we do this? How can we learn to take less interest in trying to get a patient to understand where we are coming from and show more interest in first learning to understand him or her? Before we subject the patient to a data dump and unload the litany of information about their condition or treatment, we should be familiar with the patient's background, and understand how much he or she already knows, instead of relating from a limited role. In this way, we relate from a more open, authentic self.

In vulnerable situations, patients and their families need more than just linear information, data, and evidence. They need someone who is present, and often that person is either the healthcare provider or the family care provider. We are the ones in attendance when a patient or a family is most isolated and in need of human contact. For many people, it is hard to know how to handle such depths of feeling and the neediness that goes along with this vulnerability. However, as much as our patients require the modern construct of evidence-based medicine, they also require compassion. And it is out of our compassionate connection that we will find the sacredness in these connections.

A more medically relevant story is that of the intensive care nurse in chapter 4 who compulsively took the vitals on a stable patient. By the patient's questions, she realized that it was her compulsivity in the situation that worried the patient, not his actual condition. This is an illustration of a patient pointing out an awareness that, if taken by the healthcare provider, could expand the practitioner's level of connection.

When you feel as if you cannot see past your workload to connect with this awareness, remember this story:

Mind Over Matter

A farmer woke one morning and noticed his donkey was gone. Soon, he heard the donkey's familiar bray. He walked toward the noise and found his donkey had fallen into an old, unmarked well on his property. He tried every way he could to get the donkey out, but the well was too deep. After much thought, he decided to put the screaming donkey out of its misery. He got a shovel and started throwing dirt into the well. In fact, the donkey screams became louder and filled with panic. But after a few shovels of dirt fell, the farmer noticed the donkey's screams subsided.

After the farmer tossed quite a lot of dirt into the well, the donkey jumped out. When he asked the donkey what happened, the donkey said, "After my initial panic, I decided to just shake it off and step up."

We have all had times when a patient was just the next requisite task instead of a potential connection or teacher. The patient has become an object instead of a subject. Times exist when we simply put on an attentive expression while hoping it is not obvious to a patient that we are far removed from what they are saying and needing to get on to some other task.

The Biblical tale of Mary and Martha illustrates that Martha remains busy and is operating out of her own incessant need to be needed, thus, she misses what Mary and Jesus are sharing in a holy encounter just by being present and available.

Expanded Compassion

It is difficult to simply be present with patients in certain situations. For most of us, it is still quite challenging to deliver bad news. The heightened emotions aroused in these encounters can cause discomfort and awkwardness. That discomfort may be caused by feeling responsible for the tears shed. We must learn to avoid personalizing the reaction that we get from a patient. Not injecting our sense of self into every situation takes time and some helpful guides. We need to be taught how to be present with our patients and remain in an expanded state of compassion, instead of personalizing their experiences and therefore narrowing the communication.

With this understanding, or this "standing under" the experience of another without standing in it, we shift into a new way of being able to help others because we get out of our own way.

Beyond the Personal

Frequently, it can deepen an interaction just to think about how a certain patient makes you feel. This awareness can help you see past your personal emotional injection into an encounter. Once we learn how not to insert ourselves into situations that have nothing to do with us, we will be in a better place to help patients examine their suffering. How do we remove our projected sense of self and just allow what is to be what is? This form of connection opens a whole new realm of interactions with patients.

After sharing a diagnosis and its treatment options, some patients will ponder, pause, and ask, "What would you do in this situation?" Most of us have been trained, in our two-dimensional, giver/receiver model, to say, "I have no idea what I would do, as I am not in this situation," or "I don't have a child, so I don't know how I would respond." That is the easy way out—sinking back into our objectivity and not even trying to make a connection or cognitive leap. Obviously, we are not in their situation, but is that really their question? Or are they perhaps trying to get us to join in a more compassionate and heartfelt conversation? The patient is asking us to change our clinical mind-set; inviting us to join with them, spiritually and emotionally, in their distress and in their decision. They are summoning us out of our detached preoccupation with information into a place where we reach the roots of our human connection.

In folklore and even shamanism, shape-shifters are beings with the ability to become anyone or anything. We can develop empathy by shape-shifting and asking, "What if we were that patient with a cancer diagnosis or the parent of a dying baby? What would it feel like to be them? How would we cope? What would we do next?" We need to meet the request for connection (with all the professionally appropriate qualifiers) and answer as directly as we can. If we do not, we are setting up a situation where a human being can ask a sincere question that we dismiss as a mere distraction from the singular purpose of a data download. Often, the responses we give, though correct, simultaneously dismiss the deeper question and connection that is being requested.

Thus, that perfected professional distance that we were taught becomes an obstacle to connecting to the patient. Narrowing that professional distance takes some skill and it also takes a willingness to grow past that professional detachment that no patient really enjoys. It is at times like these, when we are almost forced by a patient to shift our professional bedrock of detachment. These can be seen as times when our patients reveal our disconnection and open us up. Once we learn this, we can then offer this gift back to our patients. Some patients, especially the seriously ill, may be surrounded with well-meaning family and friends who do not have the knowledge or emotional understanding to truly minister to the sick person. Sometimes we have to be aware of the keys people need to help open them up.

The Recognizable Key
A Hmong family from Thailand came to the United States and, shortly after arriving, had a baby that was extremely premature. The world of neonatology is a very gentle world and expectations run high. Most people in our culture are programmed to expect the perfect, Gerber baby, and it often takes some doing to get these expectations down to a level consistent with reality, yet still allow for hope. This child had large, bilateral, Grade 4 brain bleeds and the treating team discussed with the parents the potential need to change from taking the intensive-care approach to stopping medical care altogether. But even after the bleeds worsened, the parents adamantly refused to even consider the possibility of stopping medical care.

Daily meetings occurred with the parents as well as the Hmong elders. Finally, a nurse, her insight coming out of her willingness to sit back and wait until something deeper could arise from her intuition, said, "You know, they are probably Buddhist and they may feel that if their child does not contribute something of value in this life, he is destined to return to a worse karma. Perhaps if you could offer them something like organ donation or some way they could feel their child had contributed something, things might change."

With few options left other than an ethics-service consultation, the treating team decided to give this a try. At the time, however, no one used any organs from a premature baby for transplantation. But there was a study underway using corneas for research, so this was offered to the family. Without even looking at each other, the mother and father both said yes immediately and agreed to discontinue medical support. They both may have been looking for a key and it was not even something they understood. But when it was presented, they both simultaneously recognized it.

In the tender world of neonatology, parents are vital constituents, and from time to time, we have to resuscitate the parents. To do this, it is crucial to try to tune into their thought processes and, as illustrated, it is helpful to know the differences between our belief systems. Religion is an important support system for most people. These underlying world views or assumptions are often fundamental in decision making and should be deeply understood. It has been said there are no atheists in foxholes, and atheists are equally rare around a deathbed. Our patients may have a different language, a different culture, or a different view of life, which comes with a radically different conceptual framework.

Every family has its own unique blend of culture and spirituality. Understanding them can be difficult and may require a different type of listening. But by listening to their questions, we can discover their foundational beliefs quite quickly. In the final analysis, the above story does not just apply to Buddhists. All parents want to feel their child's life was of value. They need to know what we have learned from their child and know our experience, the love we have seen from their family, or the inspiration we have felt because of them.

Creating a New Context

Years ago at an art museum in Santa Monica, California, an exhibit demonstrated this very well. Spread around a large, warehouse-size museum were chronologically arranged pictures of someone's childhood, through adolescence, and then to rows and rows of memorabilia, including sex paraphernalia. Visitors progressed through graphic photos of sadomasochist sexual encounters and other scenes that created either disconnection or disgust. At the end of the photo montage, there was an open door into a room. This small room, right in the middle of the art museum, was done up like a hospital room, a patient (the artist) was lying in bed with his mother at his side. He was hooked up to IVs and was in the process of dying from AIDS. The room was windowless, but the door was open; the idea seemingly being that a viewer would enter. Few could bring themselves to go in. At this point a visitor was overheard saying to her friend, "How do doctors do this? Enter the room of a complete stranger and begin a conversation or deliver some bad news. That has to be one of the hardest things. I cannot imagine doing that even in the convenient abstraction of this museum."

The awkwardness of this encounter was dramatically revealed in this performance piece. To enter the artist's room, or his world, a person had to find a place inside them beyond the contraction of fear. Viewers had to get out of self-focus and discomfort and extend themselves. Entering his isolation was a gesture of compassion that few could muster, but this skill can be learned or improved upon, especially if this compassion is innately part of one's character.

We have the ability to create a new context for our experience as well as that of our patients. The next time we enter a room and begin interacting with a patient, we need to remind ourselves that, on some level, this person is not our patient but our teacher or guru. This perspective is always available to us. We can see that this person has come to us at this specific point in our lives to teach us something that we could not learn as well from any other person or situation. Remember, a role-based healer thinks she or he is giving something to patients, but does not recognize the implicit reciprocity that is always accessible. The healer can receive something that is equally desirable and healing.

A Shift in Communication

A physician tells of a time when a mother showed up quite late for an appointment. She had a 4:30 PM appointment, the last of the day. The office closed at 5 PM. At 4:50 PM, the physician told his nurse to reschedule the patient, if she arrived. The woman arrived five minutes later. After doing some paperwork, the doctor left the office around 5:30 PM and noticed the patient with three young children sitting at the bus stop near his office. In a nonverbal way, he listened to her story. The reality of her circumstance made him embarrassed. All her effort to get there, the possibility that the bus was late, and many other things ran through his mind; his feeling of guilt clashed with the physical comfort of his sedan. A compassion he had not previously accessed was exposed.

He said he would never forget that embarrassment he felt within himself. This woman cut through something very deep within his soul; she became his teacher and he got the lesson. He went on to say that he was never going to allow something like that to happen again, in either his professional or personal life. This tardy patient unknowingly became his guru, healing him of the strict temporal linearity of his day.

In a truly conscious encounter, or in a divine appointment, both parties can receive healing. This sharing can be expanded even beyond the scope of this book to deeper and deeper mystical levels.

I Am That
Jesus, amidst some rather awe-inspiring healings, seemed to find what might be the greatest miracle—the concept that there is no separation. In effect, we are expanding the concept of, "Do unto others as you would have others do unto you," because on some level, we have discovered that they *are* us. When we look into things deeply, we are exhilarated by the recognition of our shared humanity, seeing ourselves in every patient. In the Jewish Kabala, this compassionate connection with others is described as, "When you meet someone whose story is yours, the soul is healed."

Poet Octavia Paz describes a place where "Nothing human is foreign to me." To recognize ourselves in another, or in another's situation, dissolves our separate sense of self, and allows the fullness of our soul's compassion to manifest. Our emotional heart becomes enriched with the oxygen of our spirit.

Healing Stories
People want to tell their story even if they do not appear to. We often find ourselves and our patients repeating stories. This is a part of the healing process. There are two parts to healing: telling the story and finding the meaning. The compulsive reiteration of the same story over and over with an anguished redundancy continues until someone, hopefully us, can help the person find a different meaning or a different context for their experience. Our job is to nurture people so they can discover the meaning. Otherwise, people stay stuck in their story.

For example, here is a story that may not be true, but can be very helpful to offer to mothers who have made the difficult decision to abort or who may spontaneously miscarry, in order to alleviate the guilt that is often conflated with their grief.

Things Happen for a Reason

A mother, who had had two previous abortions, and her now three-year-old daughter were sitting at the table drawing when the child spontaneously asked, "Mommy, why was it that I had to come two times before this before I could be born?"

The mother, needless to say, was speechless.

Many of us feel that things happen for a reason or that we are born under some code or agreement. If that is the case, maybe life is wiser than we are. Maybe that child decided to choose that mother as a parent and maybe the mother decided to choose this experience of having a preterm infant. A new option in thought can help relieve a mother's guilt by creating a different narrative than the one that is usually obsessively playing in a guilt-ridden mind. What is going to happen will happen, but if she can be in the best place to lovingly mother this child either in utero or ex utero, all the better.

We can plant something in our patients' healing trajectory that will give their recurrent story a boost in its search for meaning. A change in a story can act like a medication. It can go to the source of a thought, a thought virus, and be the antidote for healing. In the warmth of a genuine, caring connection, we have the ability to help change the story and work with it and even move beyond it. In the end, we hope they will find gratitude for a lesson learned instead of wallowing in the grief of a story reiterated over and over again.

Stuck in Our Story

This book stems from this same idea. We are trying to change stuck patterns in medicine by changing the way we tell the story. This, as with our patients, can expand the possible meanings that we can find. When we find this ability for ourselves, for our stories, we will find for others this new interpretive framework. Helping others to get the larger view, or the meta-view, of a lesson is truly deep healing. That is being a meta-physician or a meta-nurse in the truest sense.

Authenticity

A Buddhist concept holds that as we deepen our oneness with our true nature, we expand our compassion. This expansion into our deeper oneness—or as some say, our authentic self—is quite a shift from our role-based behaviors. This is the beginning of our professional healing, which is often jumpstarted by our patients. Frequently, we need the reflection of another because we never get pushed far enough to explore this authenticity alone.

We are privileged to be at some of life's places where authenticity is front and center, without any masks. Few people, if any, discuss their car payment or next appliance purchase on their death bed. Being with a patient who is angst-ridden about his or her death forces a different level of contemplation. It is our privilege to be around this state of consciousness.

Many spiritual traditions have ways of trying to hold consciousness in a prolonged awareness of death or transience. Some Catholic monks actually sleep in caskets to get to this awareness. Buddhists meditate over corpses, revealing the transitory nature of life. Hindu *sadus* have a staged cremation of themselves in order to let go of their former role. Being close to death is one of those rare places in life when people get truly authentic. Ill or dying patients are so honest and direct that an undeniable genuineness emerges. Sometimes, the most hardened drug addict can say something so poetic that we are immeasurably grateful for being there to hear their sharing. Often, we get to see parts of our patients we could not discover in any other context. Here we have the opportunity to share the deepest part of our humanity. This participation, this presence, which is a form of love, is something so unrestrained that it opens us to an expansiveness and an undeniable honesty within ourselves.

To be truly present, we have to be genuine enough to speak directly to that authenticity in our patient, address it, and not drag them back into the trivialities of life. Otherwise we end up with what we call "death, American-style," with its flowers, balloons, and the TV on in the room as we spout platitudes and banalities about death with exaggerated sympathy. It is easy to unintentionally become one of those irritating people who have no idea when to say nothing.

In the book *When Bad Things Happen to Good People*, Rabbi Harold Kushner describes how painful it was for him to hear the empty words people offered, which were intended to make him feel better, when his son was dying. Even more painful was his recognition that for twenty years, he had been saying the same things to other people in similar situations. It is essential to find a place where we can listen to the language of tears, a place where we are not afraid of silence. Pascal Blanchard, a famous historian and the founder of the Association Connaissance de l'histoire de l'Afrique contemporaine, observed, "All of man's problems stem from his inability to sit in a room quietly by himself." This type of listening requires a certain kind of knowing, a knowing of a depth within ourselves. This silence helps us to match the authenticity of the patient who is delving deeper and deeper into his or her authentic being. When we do not show up with our authentic self when the patient needs it, we miss a valuable opportunity to match life's deepest offering.

In our hospital environment, the most powerful therapeutic intervention we might be able to offer for the family is openness and awareness so they have a chance to find a deep experience of healing amidst the dying process. If we can be truly present, the situation will then instruct our life as well.

Healthcare providers frequently feel guilty about not doing everything possible even when it does not make medical sense to do so. If nothing more can be done medically, helping the patient get to the point of acceptance can be a deep healing. We rarely think of the spiritual and emotional additions we can add to a situation when, in actuality, this may be the most meaningful, profound thing we can do.

Stuck Energy

It is rare that someone in our culture can hold the mystery of not knowing why something has occurred for any period of time. A mother who goes into preterm labor often feels a secret shame, a tremendous sense of guilt for playing golf the day before, having had sex the night before, or having taken her prenatal yoga class. All of these are ways of trying to find an answer, trying to control things cognitively.

This brings about that same stuck pattern as a repetitious story. Many times, guilt is a form of control. We are so used to having control that when something like death happens, outside our control, it is easier to find that control by assessing blame. Guilt is a way of blaming ourselves just as suing the doctor, the nurse, or the hospital is a way of projecting fault. These experiences give us, as a healthcare worker, a spiritual invitation.

Anyone in intensive care knows this story: When a patient gets to the point where the family has to decide about a Do Not Resuscitate (DNR), often those closest to the patient (the spouse, the children, or others with a close connection) already know the person's wishes and having done all they need to do in their grieving, can allow the person to go. But the sibling of a patient, or a child who has not spoken to the parent for a year or two due to some unresolved issue, often arrives and adamantly refuses to agree to stop the life-support technology. Maybe that fear encapsulated in guilt is a contraction that cannot allow for a different narrative until we can see into it and then open it up for our patients.

Seeing this happen repeatedly shows how guilt or anger often blocks our ability to let a relative go. Grief is prolonged when there is guilt or when our connection is somehow ambivalent. How we deal with someone's death is colored by the connection we had in life. If we could see how guilt can be an obstacle to releasing and then heal it in ourselves as caregivers, we will have created a new awareness to share with our patients. Try, if possible, to remove the blocks of guilt from someone's progression on the path of grief.

Bearing Witness

In some situations, all we can do is bear witness to the suffering of another. All we can do is provide a safety net and a space so that the sufferers know they will not be abandoned. Instead of encountering someone who is trying to change them, or someone who merely hands them a Kleenex and pats them on the back with the hope of stopping their crying, patients meet an accepting spaciousness in their healer—a stillness that is a clear mirror in which to observe their own reactive entanglement. We reflect back another possibility, an authenticity they can find, a resonance with our being that offers them another prospect through the tone of our voice, or maybe just our quiet body language. This quality of the heart can be developed and can maintain a connection whether with words, tears, anger, or silence. Some things require no speech—they are infused or reflected from one heart to another by just staying present and available.

We see this powerfully illustrated in the story of Jesus in the Garden of Gethsemane. Jesus asked his disciples to stay with him and not abandon him while he prayed in the garden. This was a simple request, but none of them could fulfill it. It is at times like these when we truly find out if we are in medicine to help others and if we are ministering to their deepest needs, or if we are operating out of our own limitations.

Inner Resources

When it comes to these types of spiritual understandings, we cannot share a message that we have not received and integrated into our own life. As our patients teach us about the inner resources of our soul, we begin to more clearly see those same resources in the patients and families who come to us. At first this can be a rather existentially disorganizing phenomenon for our role-based behaviors, but it is also the initiation of a deepening in our profession; a time when we begin to understand what supports people by having witnessed it in our own experience. This awareness is what determines the quality of our presence, helping patients and their families become multifaceted; listening, digging deeply into what they have said, pulling out the helpful insights, emphasizing them, and then mixing those ingredients together to shine light on a new perspective.

We can be truly compassionate by letting our patients experience their illness in the unique way that arises from their individual personalities and from their connection with us. This type of presence, this altar between two people, or just having this sacred intention underneath our actions, is what can then be felt by a patient. When we do not arrive in the fullness of our authentic potential with a loving intention, we fail the patient and ourselves.

Love

In the healing process we are privileged to discover something more real and authentic in the depths of ourselves. Many of us have never learned to successfully penetrate into a patient's crisis deeply enough, but once we do, if we are truly present in this type of conversation, we will be shaped by it. We obtain the rich spiritual paychecks of our profession when every act is attended to with love and devotion. As a Hindi guru says, "If it is not done with love, it is dust."

Showing up with love allows a continued deepening of our contemplative spirituality. However, we must realize that the lessons, or opportunities, may come in disguise. Our patients and co-workers show up in an endless array of costumes, and it takes a bit of a mental excursion to create the new awareness in which to see the blessings in the midst of the disguise. In *Beyond Words*, Sri Swami Satchidananda tells a story that expresses reinventing one's expectations and perceptions:

Blessings in Disguise

There was a man a long time ago who prayed every day, "God, I really want You to come in person, to have a nice sumptuous lunch with me." Because he was constantly nagging, God appeared one day and said, "Okay, I'll come."

"God," he said, "I am so happy, when can you come? You must give me time to prepare everything." God replied, that He would come on Friday at noon. Before He left, the man asked if he could invite all his friends. God said, sure and then disappeared. When the clock chimed at noon, the man was puzzled that God was not punctual, so he waited another half hour. The guests began telling him that he was a fool. Why would God come have lunch with him anyway, they shouted. The man walked inside and saw a big black dog on the dining room table, eating everything there. *Oh, no*, the man thought, *that is why God did not come; he sensed a dog eating all his food.* He started beating the dog with a club, and the dog cried and ran away. He felt so bad, he went back and prayed. Finally, God appeared to him again, but there were wounds and bandages all over his body.

"What happened?" asked the man, "you must have gotten into a terrible accident."

"It was no accident," God said, "it was you."

"Why do you blame me?" said the man.

"Because I came punctually at noon and started eating. Then you came and beat me. You clubbed me and broke my bones."

"But you didn't come," said the man.

"Are you sure nobody was eating your food?"

"Well, yes, there was a big black dog."

"Who is that, then if not me? I really wanted to enjoy your food, so I came as a dog," said God.

We are being offered these opportunities on a daily basis. Do we have the refreshed eyes to see them?

A Graced Awakening

This grounding in the spirituality needed for our profession is a graced awakening. Once we get to the point of seeing that the healer is not one particular person in the room, but the meeting itself, our patients can then teach us how to be a blessing in their lives. Our days will have a renewed sense of awe because we never really know what can happen when we approach our work from this perspective. As we become more present, we will develop new areas of awareness that will deepen into new levels of connection and witnessing for our patients. On a more mystical level, we develop a passion to extend our understanding beyond the patient in front of us and better understand our shared humanity. In the next chapter, we will explore how we can discover and cultivate this same awareness in our connection and communication with our co-workers.

Chapter 7
Healing Relationships with Our Co-Workers

"Each friend represents a world within us, a world possibly not born until they arrive, and it is only by this meeting that a new world is made."
—Anais Nin

Many find that one of the most difficult things in healthcare is not so much dealing with the patients as dealing with our co-workers. Improving those interpersonal relationships is a needed step before we can heal healthcare, either individually or collectively. Interpersonal pollutants often create a toxic microenvironment in healthcare that lingers even after the macroenvironment has improved. Co-workers and their attitudes have a great deal to do with the climate in which you work. In this chapter, we will focus on how we interact with our co-workers.

Strength and the Boy
A boy and his father were walking along a road when they came across a large stone. The boy said to his father, "Do you think if I use all my strength, I can move this rock?" His father answered, "If you use all your strength, I am sure you can do it." The boy began to push the rock. Exerting himself as much as he could, he pushed and pushed. The rock did not move. Discouraged, he said to his father, "You were wrong. I can't do it." His father placed his arm around the boy's shoulder and said, "No son. You didn't use all your strength. You didn't ask me to help."

Current healthcare practices often have us identifying with the son because we are accustomed to doing everything ourselves. Co-workers can become respected collaborators, best friends, second families, or the reason you look for another job. Everyone wants to feel needed and inspired at work, yet many of us miss the opportunities for growth and inspiration that daily interactions could offer. How, then, do we develop for our wounded, oft-suffering co-workers the levels of compassion and reciprocal healing we have for our patients?

As we have learned in previous chapters, our patterns and roles can become obstacles to the awareness of the healing potential between us. Frequently, we find ourselves enmeshed in the frenetic energy of the hospital environment—anxiously running around, rarely even having time for lunch, much less time to connect with our co-workers. When our focus is so scattered, effectively combining the strengths of men and women who share a passion for healing can be difficult. Roles often unite us from a collapsed place of weakness instead of encouraging us to find our greater combined strengths, such as the father did in the above story.

Beginnings

We need to develop an awareness of how we interact with others. We will not be able to change the workplace until we see the potential value that can result from a different level of interaction.

Our co-workers are our karma, our mirrors. As mentioned in an earlier chapter, life may be sending us relationships that are perfect for healing our wounds and we do not want to miss the opportunity to be touched and transformed by them. We must learn to not only notice these offerings, but see them as opportunities for spiritual practice. Do not miss the opportunities when presented—big or small. They are offered constantly in the course of our work day if we choose to view them this way.

The complex interactions in our stressful work environment can trigger the full range of our emotions. These emotional triggers can offer clues to places in us we may want to look for development or healing. For example, it is easy to feel compassion for a patient who is destitute, but for a colleague suffering in prosperity, we may be less able to feel compassion. To have to listen to the continual problems of someone with a grand home can be challenging, especially if you do not care all that much about the carpet color in your own home, much less having to hear daily about theirs.

We may also lack the skills to raise the conversation to another level. The Bible tells us, "In the beginning was the Word." That is not just the beginning of the universe; it is the beginning of everything we do. We need to recognize the potential creative power of our conversations.

Eric's Communication: Isolating vs. Bonding

In the first week of medical school, Eric repeatedly found himself in conversations with other students about how hard school was, how the tests were oppressive, and how this life change was so narrowing. The theme was always how difficult medical school was. Fortunately, Eric was not full of the same complaints. He had not yet lost sight of the privilege of just getting into medical school. Having several friends who had been accepted gave him a different perspective. But as time went on, he lost touch with his former college friends and was enmeshed within the circles of his new medical colleagues.

He remembered, early on, wanting to say, "We've only been here a few days! How can this intense complaining already be happening?" But, after a time, he realized that this complaining was actually a form of bonding. Whenever he tried to point out how fortunate they all were, or that they had only been in school for a week and hadn't even had an exam yet, he saw that he would gradually be excluded from connecting with other students.

As he progressed in his career, he noticed at the beginning of his residency that others were already complaining about the workload and call schedule. Again he thought, "How could this already be happening? We've only been here three days and most of us haven't even had a call night yet." But, once again, he kept quiet, knowing that his sharing would only separate him from the group connection. Gradually, he began to join in the dialogue, divorcing himself from his deeper truth in order to remain connected.

Over time, Eric realized what was happening. Whenever he was in a new group of physicians, and later in his career with a new group of nurses at lunch in the cafeteria, the easiest or fastest way to bond with others seemed to be through sharing mutual gripes. The pattern of "I'll go along with your story if you'll go along with mine" was a powerful way of connecting. The collective pattern of bonding through negativity was a way to access a quick connection, even to the point where Eric realized that validating a woman's complaint about a co-worker led to more dates. After a time, though, Eric wasn't sure if those were the dates he wanted. He had grown bored with this level of conversation and was ready for a change.

Eric, like many of us, lacked the skill to enter a conversation and stabilize a higher level of connection. It was easier to stay with the complaints, than try to transform what was being shared. Again, this book is an example of trying to change these connections on a collective level. Perhaps, one of the reasons it is so difficult to change collective behavior is because it requires us to challenge some of our usual patterns and go against what may be considered the status quo. Like Eric, we acquiesce in these patterns in some of our first interactions in healthcare. Imagine changing that dynamic. Wouldn't it be great to know that your co-workers were really there to help you find the freedom to access your dreams, not to encourage and support stagnation? This is illustrated by a Zen story:

Frogs and the Well

Two little frogs were stuck in a deep roadside ditch. As they jumped and jumped trying to escape, many other frogs gradually circled the ditch, croaking their encouragement. Soon, it became apparent to those outside that the hole was too deep and the two little frogs would never escape. Then the encouraging nature of the many changed: "It is no use. You've tried all you can. It's hopeless."

One frog in the ditch got discouraged and stopped jumping. Totally exhausted, he collapsed in fatigue. The second frog kept jumping and jumping. The encircled frogs continued yelling to him that it was hopeless. After what seemed like hours, the second frog succeeded in jumping out of the ditch.

Stunned, the other frogs asked, "How did you do that? None of us thought you could make it. We were all telling you to give up." The little frog blinked and said, "Oh, I'm hard of hearing and couldn't understand exactly what you were saying. I thought you were encouraging me to keep trying."

Loosening the emotional habit of focusing on the negative, may allow us to succeed like the frog in this story.

Energy Drains

We often get good at telling stories, or gossiping, if you will. Our co-workers dump their professional opinions and personal garbage on us just as we do to them. This is a way of dealing with an issue by externalizing the energy needed to effect a change rather than internalizing it and looking within. Unfortunately, gossiping is basically throwing away the energy, even though it may decrease stress by venting.

A more universal example might be to notice that we, as a country, are addicted to the tabloids. Why is that? Maybe it is because when our lives cease to be contemplative and spiritual in focus, conversations can easily degenerate into mere gossip. The creative energy that we are not using has to go somewhere.

As time passes, and our first moments as a nurse or doctor fade into a stream of long days and nights, we find ourselves no longer discussing our hopes and visions with others. Instead, we jump into the quickest way to connect: complaining. When we are tired or fearful, it is much easier to establish relationships built on the easy commonality of dislikes and disinterest rather than investing time in developing relationships built on trust. So we gripe about how demanding the doctors are or how clueless the administration is. We discuss the passive-aggressive or active-aggressive ward clerk's latest tactic, how annoying a patient is, or why we are so irked by the overtime policy. Relationships based on a bond forged in complaints and gossip are weak and destructive. Is it any wonder mutual healing cannot thrive in this atmosphere?

Instead of persisting with collective complaints or gossip, we need to find other outlets for our suppressed creative energies. If we learn how to stabilize a higher level of consciousness in a group, we will be surprised how fast we can bring others up to our level of thinking and how appreciative our co-workers will be. People want to bond on higher levels, but they often lack the skills or the examples of how to achieve this.

Listening for Compliments

One simple technique to help transform a relatively stuck negative energy at work is to listen throughout the day for compliments. When we hear someone say something positive about someone or something, make sure to repeat it to the person or, better yet, perhaps share it with the person in front of a group at lunch. This breaks the pattern of negativity and places the conversation on another trajectory. This sort of sharing also encourages others to follow suit.

Nurturing our co-workers is not something we learn in school. The word "education" derives from the Latin *educare*, meaning to draw forth from within. In our culture, however, education often comes to mean to pound in from without. Most of us develop in systems based more on competition than collaboration. Our educational system's way of communicating is not the most nurturing model for molding healthy collaboration.

The truth is we are all imperfect and most of us feel incompetent at some level in our jobs. There is so much to know these days that few, if any, of us develop the confidence that we have completed our knowledge base. But if we always keep our focus on our supposed lack, we end up feeling insecure. Why keep the focus there when we have other options for supporting and nurturing people? Let's begin to include in our evaluations and assessments of students and co-workers the spiritual qualities of compassion and presence as well as assessments of their technical skills.

Competition vs. Collaboration

The first day of nursing school should be a happy, congratulatory time in one's life. Yet the opening speech at one particular school on the first day was, "Look around you. Look left and look right. One out of three of you will not be here on graduation day. You all have a lot of work ahead of you."

Instead of a congratulatory embrace for having jumped through all the hoops correctly to get into a school of nursing, the school sends a message of competition and fear right from the start.

Without a nurturing context, a student can lose the most important reference point: what lies within. A teacher who can guide a student toward his or her inner wisdom and compassion is one who can further the student's long-term development. We can do the same in later years with our co-workers by sharing compliments and reflections with them on things we see in them and value.

Unfortunately, higher education is rarely about the inner life and developing potential. We seldom get lectures discussing how to enjoy and deepen our experience in healthcare. And our workplace interactions often mirror this same limitation.

The Dermatologist's Awareness

A dermatologist, reflecting at a seminar, stated, "I went through eight years of medical education and honestly can't recall anyone ever asking me how I felt. I got the message that feelings were simply not considered important, that they were not included in the standardized way to think.

"I was trained to be directed by others, rather than to be in contact with myself. I remember at the end of my first year in residency thinking, 'What about me?' I felt so lost. I could keep up the pace and I felt like I was doing a great job, but sometimes it would hit me that I was just a rat on a wheel. As long as I stayed up in my head and ignored my feelings, I was fine. But it didn't pass me by during my rotations to notice that dermatologists seemed to be one of the rare specialties where people are happy. They seemed much more aware of the need for self care. They had decent hours and kept that as a priority. Needless to say, I'm in Derm."

Stressing Efficiency

Most of us were trained in schools that stressed efficiency over nurturance. We end up becoming time hogs, rarely assessing the effectiveness of our interactions because of our focus on efficiency. We end up frequently dissatisfied with ourselves. If we complete rounds by noon or finish our morning assessments by 8:30 AM, we think that maybe we could have finished sooner. The dynamic of impatience in many of our interactions tends to block us from the awareness of the divine appointments that encircle our days.

Buddhists have an expression, "Haste is a form of violence." Haste is not only violent to others, but a form of violence to ourselves and our developing potential. We need to slow down enough to allow our patients and our co-workers to tell their stories without interruption. This allows us a simultaneous spaciousness to enter into our own story. It can be a listening point in our day where we can focus on effectively integrating our own healing, instead of running around trying to solve the problems of everyone else and, in the end, avoiding the reality of our own wounds and need for healing.

Nurturing Education

These issues need to be recognized. Otherwise, like Eric, we become passive victims of our educational environment long after we graduate. If we take responsibility for our collective dynamics from the inception of our careers, we can avoid becoming victims of a process whose long-term impact we can hardly appreciate. If we do not deeply question what is happening, we, and future generations of healthcare workers, end up with a foundation that keeps the current dynamics in place. Unfortunately, our educational system is not a soulful search. When you sign up for medical or nursing school, self-development is put on hold, and it usually remains that way in your work day and sometimes even throughout your professional career.

Frank's Pursuit of Continuing Education

Frank was set up on a blind date with Randy. Frank's friends explained that they always thought he dated people who were not up to his level. Now they claimed to have found the perfect guy. Randy and Frank were both physicians. Their friends felt they would have a lot in common. Unfortunately, Frank found that Randy spent the whole first date (the last date, by the way) complaining about the problems with healthcare. This wasn't Frank's biggest gripe. His biggest gripe happened to be people who spend all of their time complaining about the healthcare system. Not a heavenly match. It became apparent to Frank that Randy's education and creative explorations had stopped once he got his diploma.

After the date, when his friends asked how it went, Frank said, "I really appreciate the introduction, but to be honest I think I'd rather date a high school dropout who's interested in reading and continuing to learn instead of someone who spends his evenings repeating workplace dysfunctions. The guy thought he was so insightful, but didn't share one interesting perspective that I hadn't heard a hundred times before."

Frank can feel upset, as many of us do at work, or he can try to develop the skills to draw others into a more conscious conversation. If he chooses, Frank could see this date as a divine appointment—a gift. We all have people at work like Randy, the complainer.

We can only hope that a few people in our workplace drive us crazy. We all have those dreaded button-pushers in our workday. These relationships often end up being our *koans*, the unsolvable problems we have to live with and try to learn to look at with new eyes each day. Some of these people are as hard-hitting in their persona as the whack of a Zen master's stick. In the Zen tradition, the master will do anything to get one's attention and deepen it, from knocks on the head, to yelling at or completely ignoring someone. Who are the koans of your work day?

We all know people who drain our energy. These irritators can be great teachers. They can help us learn how to stop tremendous drains of health and emotion that stem from conflicts and confusion.

The relationships most bothersome to us usually signal the deepest place of our limitations, areas of interpersonal infection that we take to many other parts of life. These situations are worth focusing on. It is easy to make the mistake of letting our mood, instead of our highest potential, determine how we respond to others. Your curiosity and contemplation of these koans, once they are made conscious, not only deserve to be respected but will be rewarded.

Your Most Personal Ally

In chapter 5, you were asked to recall the person who most irritates you. More than likely, he or she was a co-worker. This is the person who usually ends up playing the bad cop, with you as the good cop or victim, in many of your workplace stories. Take a minute to think about this person. What is it about him or her that is so exasperating?

According to Buddhists, the person who aggravates and antagonizes us the most is seen as our greatest teacher. As mentioned earlier, Buddhists call this the Near-Enemy Practice. It encourages us to have immense gratitude for this "enemy" because our continual struggles with them prod our growth. This may be a stretch, but what is there to lose by trying this suggestion? For one day, or just one hour, pretend that this person is your most powerful ally in your personal deepening. You will immediately have to change your perspective on this person—now honoring him or her and embracing with gratitude the struggles this near enemy brings.

As the saying goes, we must "keep our friends close and our enemies closer." But we are not keeping our enemies close in order to keep an eye on them, we are actually going to learn to harvest the negative energy that is produced when we come into contact with this person. When we repeatedly react with intensity to a co-worker's traits, we can learn to turn that inquiry inward. Usually, we will find those traits correspond directly to a part of us or our past, some parental dynamic, sibling conflict, or other thing that we have denied, disowned, or otherwise lost.

The Bible challenges, "I tell you: Love your enemies and pray for those who persecute you." (Matthew 5:44–45). Whether in prayer or meditation, we should consider the personal contemplative practice of learning the lessons offered from those who persecute us.

When we begin to look at our co-workers differently and observe encounters with a more developed spiritual awareness, we begin to notice those parts of us that are wounded and are causing restricted patterns of relating. Integrating our near enemy, as well as other co-workers, in our spiritual practice at work can be a great way to facilitate our own healing. Paying attention to how a person triggers our negative reactions is just the first step. Tracing our behaviors back to a general pattern we have in relating can bring an awareness that can free us from the stagnant, limiting pattern.

Dr. McGully's Human Homework

Dr. McGully frequently spent a large part of his morning complaining about the disproportionate burden of the call schedule he was forced to share. But on the occasions when his supervisor stepped in the room, there were only tangential comments made, such as, "Dr. Coleman, could you please bring my mail down from the office? I never seem to have time to get up there to get it."

One day, after several of these rather passive-aggressive comments,

Dr. Coleman laid it out for Dr. McGully. "If you're trying to tell me something indirectly, just so you know, I prefer the direct route. And if you can't be direct with me, let me be so with you. If you look at the call schedules, you'll notice that you have exactly the same number, amount, and proportion of calls as everyone else in this group. You're treated with a ridiculous level of equality, based on my desire for everything to be fair. So if this job is too much for you, or you feel this is more than you can handle without complaining or doling out these side comments, I'll be happy to make sure you get placed somewhere else. Again, I'd prefer you be as direct with me as I try to be with you."

With that, Dr. McGully was taken back. He began to respond, "Well, my previous boss ..." and proceeded to give a litany of characteristics he thought a boss should possess. Dr. Coleman respectfully responded that he was not his previous boss, and that he was not even remotely like him.

Dr. McGully had spent his life having trouble with authority figures, projecting onto them dynamics from past woundings with his father. Once Dr. Coleman confronted him, Dr. McGully had to take a different look at which came first: the unfair supervisor or his perception that all authority figures were unfair. Often awareness like Dr. McGully's can be curative.

The homework being offered here is to observe the difficult parts of our co-workers and to possibly find, as Dr. McGully did, that authority figures live less in reality than in our imagination. It is said that it is "impossible to defeat an enemy who has an outpost in your head." Defeating an enemy is impossible if we are not even aware it may be in our head. Everyone has parts of their personality that invite our projections and, unfortunately, it is all too easy to think these projections are God's truth. We need to develop an awareness that allows us to distinguish our projections from objective observations.

Look at the Stories
One clue that a reaction stems from a personal projection and not an objective observation comes, as we have mentioned before, by looking at the story surrounding a situation. Are we repeating the story over and over? Is there an intensity that is almost evangelical in the emotion shared?

In previous chapters, we learned to practice limiting the amount of times we tell a story, especially a story in which we played a victim. But sometimes we cannot stop telling the story. Complaining about a situation or a person may be one way to get rid of energy, but it often is not very productive. It does not keep enough of the energy directed inward so we can transform our own inner awareness. This is the time to hold that negative energy in, to track that reaction beyond the person involved, and try to see him or her as a guide pointing us to a deeper part of our awareness, a part that needs uncovering in order to heal.

Between stimulus and response there is a space, and in that space rests our power to choose our response. Taking a moment to pause often blocks the escalation of a story. This allows us to pay attention to our own physical reaction, and gives us the space to not take something personally, or to look for some hidden meaning behind another's actions.

Many ways exist to take in a stimulus and process it. Another spiritual practice is just to find as many diverse ways of looking at a story as possible. This practice will help us and, once we completely understand it, can also be very helpful with our patients. We can help them take their stories, often the stories of their suffering, and help them expand their understandings in their search for meaning. For example, say someone steps off a corner curb and a speeding car cuts him off. This person yells, "Jerk!" Another person might think, "Gosh, I'm always in the wrong place at the wrong time." A third perspective might be, "That guy must be having a bad day." And a fourth person in a different mental space might decide, "This must be a sign that I must move out of this city." The bottom line is what we are experiencing is not as important as how we interpret the experience.

Dismantling "Buttons"

Disarming a button-pusher takes time and energy. It becomes our job and our healing to learn to dismantle the buttons that block our connection with others. Once we develop the ability to confront, investigate, and transform patterns regardless of what someone is doing to irritate us, we are on the road to transformation.

In truth, no one can make any of us feel anything unless we give them that power. We say to ourselves, "What you did triggered anger in me." We say this to ourselves to clarify that they may have acted as a trigger, but the anger is our reaction. They could have easily triggered compassion or any of a hundred other emotions. When we are sleep deprived or hungry, for example, it is much easier to take things personally or to be easily irritated with co-workers. Our state of mind and the conversations we engage in, which greatly impact our state of mind, are our responsibility.

Self-Inquiry

The self-inquiry mentioned in chapter 5 offers a useful technique of deep questioning. Questions like, "Who am I in this situation?" or "Who am I in this energy?" gets us much further on the spiritual path than the usual question, "Who does he think he is?"

By taking responsibility for our mind and conversations, we can learn to respond with compassion even when those around us behave badly. This is a form of meditation. Our co-workers become our meditation. (Warning: Letting co-workers know this tends to freak them out.) When we adopt this meditative intention, we find we can start each interaction with an attitude of openness and willingness to discover something new. With this, a new energy arises in our interactions. We find when we look at ourselves in the mirror of our relationships, every situation can be changed by activating the intention to step back, reevaluate, and reengage on a higher level of consciousness.

Take the Higher Ground

A congenitally quick-tempered male cardiologist enters the intensive care unit. With his unique brand of inquiry, he ends up offending several nurses on a consistent basis. Within minutes of his arrival, several of the ICU nurses are in tears. Interestingly enough, there are many nurses who have never had this type of encounter with him. Some even like him. One even married him.

One nurse described him by saying, "He has a form of intensity that can be easily taken personally. But his raised voice and anger is actually a form of passionate caring; you just have to be able to see through the stage show. If you don't like it, just don't give him the stage. You don't help an alcoholic by buying them a drink, and you don't help an attention junkie by feeding their drama. They are asking for something deeper. They are calling for a higher vision than the one they are stuck in. There is nothing his anger hates worse than no response at all. If he doesn't have anger, guilt, or shame to feed on, he dies out. But you have to supply that for him."

She continued, "Probably because of my family background, I've always had the ability to really listen to what is being said and not get caught up in the personality of the individual conveying the message. I grew up in a very loud Sicilian clan. This ability was hard earned; it required me to remain attentive to the feelings and reactions stirred in me so that I could be in a better position to respond to others. If you fight back, either with parents or co-workers, you often lose your power and amplify theirs. Usually people who use anger or drama are better adjusted to the chaos in their life than you are. They usually don't have much experience with any other forms of connection. Don't bother getting on their level.

"This dysfunctional mechanism of interacting is something he deals with every day, at work and at home. You'll find he appreciates someone who doesn't engage. He wants everyone around him to be in fear and he wants to control them. You have to see this as a fear-based individual whose anxieties are so overwhelming that he has to manipulate others into sharing those feelings. Fear is his familiar friend.

"Be assured that he has a very different inner reality than you. For example, you can see the way he uses sarcastic put-downs and attempts to pass them off as comedy, when it is really a way of confusing you into the same anxiety he experiences. Clearly, he needs to learn to communicate in order to relate rather than to control. But don't make it your problem."

Though this type of individual makes up an extremely small portion of the population, the emotional and energetic damage he causes is disproportionately large. But even when it is clear who really has the problem, it is still worth the time to pause and contemplate what growth may be available. We have to make our behavior about *our* well-being, not the other person's toxicity. We have two choices: Adopt the drama of the situation, or respond as the nurse above did, in a way that does not completely consume our awareness or devour our energy. We do not need to give our adversary the energetic tools to further escalate a conflict.

Lifting Up Others

To position ourselves where someone's behavior does not collapse us, we must learn to stabilize a higher level of consciousness and lift him or her up to our level. This lifting up is a form of compassion. Compassion gives us a panoramic view, whereas anger is narrow and is usually based on very little information. Anger leaves no room to treat a situation openly or creatively. Creativity comes when you start with an attitude of openness and a willingness to discover something new.

When we stabilize a more spiritual energy, it becomes more evident that, as the Dalai Lama says, everyone just wants to be happy. When we approach others with this perspective, we develop an acceptance of others that can help melt away their dysfunctions because they get no reinforcement from us. We become like tai chi masters, deflecting anger instead of impaling arrows. We gain a spaciousness that allows us to notice the emotional state of others—observing, in the moment, the way they hold their pen, or how they have tied their hair back—knowing what this tells us about the energy they bring to an encounter.

With this focus, we can show up with a refreshed awareness and a spiritual sense of peace that is palpable. People generally have a hard time sustaining anger or any other fear-based behavior in the face of this positive spiritual energy. As the nurse in the story above relayed, fears need to be fed to stay alive.

Imprisoning Others

Yet another spiritual practice mentioned in chapter 5 is to be aware of how fluid people can be. Recall that the Hindi say, "One cannot step into the same river twice." This is not merely because the river flows and changes the water every moment, but because the one who steps into the river continually changes as well. We never return to a room as exactly the same person who left.

Factual memory may hold that "this man insulted me yesterday." That thinking can become static—a way of imprisoning him in a certain mental space. We may then think we know him, but we have blocked fluidity in our knowing him with our serial judgments. On the other hand, if we bring compassion to this situation, we may allow the possibility that he might have changed. Or at least compassion honors that possibility. This allows some fresh energy into a situation, allows an infusion of a presence that refuses the stuckness of habit. Sometimes the fixed behavior we perceive in others is not theirs by nature; it is our thinking about them that keeps them in that pattern.

The Sufis have a wonderful spiritual practice regarding verbal exchanges. They feel each statement we make should pass three mental checkpoints. First, we ask ourselves, "Are these words true?" Only if they are true for both ourselves and the receiver do we ask the second question, "Are they necessary?" If, indeed, these words must be spoken, they have to pass the final test of "Are they kind?" These three questions can keep us on track with our spiritual responsiveness and let us know whether someone else is off with theirs.

A Buddhist practice is to do something kind for someone who has insulted or hurt us, and to do this kindness within one day of the insult. This places the receiver in an unexpected place and can help change the situation's energy. The Buddha said holding a grudge is like hanging on to a hot coal—you may intend to throw it at someone else, but you are the one who gets burned. From the Christian tradition, St. John of the Cross wrote, "Where you find no love, put love and you will find love." Try this creative response instead of the usual reaction. It gets energy moving in our relationships instead of the stagnation that can create an interpersonal cesspool.

Being One's Own "Near Enemy"

Some people, when asked who irritates them the most at work, respond, "Myself." Sometimes we are our own near enemy. As way to access the compassion and perspective we can often so easily give to others but not ourselves, the Hindi faith suggests trying to view an act as we would see it if it was done by someone we loved. This type of compassionate response can allow us to become more of a witness to our experience. We can create a distance where our sense of self is not automatically inserted into the narrative.

A Whole New Perspective

Our customary ways of working with our challenges—compulsions, a difficult boss, even international conflicts—do not bring the healing we long for. As we realize this, we become more open to exploring new ways of working with, learning from, and eventually being healed by what we formerly resisted and tried to control. Imagine a hospital or clinic where conversation replaces confrontation. Healthcare providers could arrive at work each day trusting that they will not be criticized, judged, or yelled at, not because this dynamic has been extinguished from the workplace, but because we have a whole new perspective.

In the spiritual text, *A Course in Miracles,* a miracle is said to occur not when a situation changes, but when we are able to change our thinking about a situation. We can expand our thinking from being a victim into knowing that we attract people into our lives for our own greatest healing. By using our relationships as conscious places for learning and growth, we activate the energy of one of life's omnipresent teachers. This perspective not only changes the way we approach relationships, it also changes our relationships into something honored instead of something dismissed through complaints.

Starting a Group

At workshops, we frequently hear that people have tried some of these techniques but have failed to change their workplace dynamics. One of the hardest things to do is to pull those around us up to a different level of dialogue and interaction. Initially, we may feel very isolated in our thinking. Spiritual traditions have acknowledged the power of a collective experience. To access change, we need to form a collective with a shared awareness.

Buddhists take refuge in, or turn to, not only the Buddha and the Dharmic principles, but also to the *sangha,* the shared community on the path of awakening. Setting up a group, or sangha, at work can be a great help on our path of spiritual deepening in the workplace.

A workplace sangha, or wisdom circle as it is called in the Native American tradition, can be a place where people come together in a spirit of friendship, where everyone can simultaneously be both student and teacher, both healer and healed. We are all familiar with the health consequences of isolation versus the research showing the benefits of being engaged in a support group. We know this is true with cancer patients, why not with the emotional cancers in our places of work? By connecting with others in groups, we find that what one person alone cannot hold on to, others can help stabilize by the synergy of mutual remembering.

Beyond starting a group, it can be helpful to designate a daily consciousness representative—someone from the group who can watch members' interactions throughout the day, and guide them if they lose their awareness to the most helpful spiritual principle. This must be done very carefully. In the midst of drama, no one appreciates someone hissing, "Shhh!" But going to someone with the intent to reflect a reaction or thought can begin to help integrate these principles in the workplace. Someone reminding us of our unconscious patterns can be done with respect and even humor, making our collective development something embraced in a creative and loving way.

Wisdom Circle Insight
One nurse in our wisdom circle mentioned an awareness she had: "When I come to work, I find there are days when everyone seems to be an ass. That's when I know I need a day off. But when only one person seems to be an ass, I know *they* need a day off. In my early years, it was quite easy to point fingers at others without noticing my own contributions to situations that drained my energy. As I mature, it becomes more and more difficult for me to overlook my own contributions to the problems at the workplace."

How do we find the people for this group? Where do we find those who want to play with refreshed awareness? We can develop a sense of recognition, similar to a Type A person recognizing another Type A person. When we observe others, they will reveal their mind-sets in the way they listen, the way they consciously progress through their day, their tone of voice, their choice of words, and the certain look of compassion in their eyes. We will sense that they have some kind of purpose in them beyond the appliance nurse or stock doc. These are the people to connect with. The time of a Lone Ranger or individual super hero is over. This waking up to our healing potential requires a collective effort. A collective wisdom can arise that has enormous power.

Sometimes the culture of a whole unit can be transformed by a small group of seekers trying to keep their workday in line with their spiritual truths. This consciousness can transform the social environment into one of more mindfulness and compassion. As with many religions, from Buddhism to Orthodox Judaism, a community is required to really stabilize collective spiritual practice. You feel supported, and not alone, because you have a larger collective sharing the same commitment. The group becomes the guru or teacher, with each person having things to share from his or her experience. As time goes on, our responses to certain situations will surprise us, and our group, as we witness a transformation from the way we usually react to a situation to the development of a more creative, responsive posture. Little in our culture teaches us how to utilize this form of collective inquiry—these types of soul interactions.

A parable from an unknown author illustrates this.

The Rabbi's Gift

A monastery had fallen upon hard times. Once a great order, cultural changes over the past few hundred years had sapped its strength. All of its branch houses were closed and there were only five monks left in the decaying mother house: the abbot and four others, all over seventy years of age. Clearly, it was a dying order.

In the deep woods surrounding the monastery was a little hut that a rabbi from a nearby town occasionally used for a hermitage. The monks could always sense when the rabbi was in the woods, and during one such visit it occurred to the abbot to pay the rabbi a visit and to ask if he might have some advice that could save the monastery.

The rabbi welcomed the abbot at his hut. But when the abbot explained the purpose of his visit, the rabbi could only commiserate with him. "I know how it is," he said. "The spirit has gone out of the people. It is the same in my town. Almost no one comes to the synagogue anymore."

So the old men wept together. They read parts of sacred scriptures and spoke quietly of deep things. When the abbot finally rose to leave, they embraced, and he asked again, "Is there nothing you can tell me to help me save my dying order?"

"No, I am sorry," the rabbi responded. "I have no advice to give. The only thing I can say is that one of you is the Messiah."

When the abbot returned to the monastery, his fellow monks gathered around him to ask, "Well, what did the rabbi say?"

"He couldn't help," the abbot answered. "We just wept and read Holy Scriptures together. Although, just as I was leaving, he did say something rather strange. He said that the Messiah is one of us. I don't know what he meant."

In the days and weeks that followed, the old monks pondered this and wondered whether there was any possible significance to the rabbi's words.

The Messiah is one of us? Could he possibly have meant one of us monks here at the monastery? If that's the case, which one? Do you suppose he meant the abbot? Yes, if he meant anyone, he probably meant Father Abbot. On the other hand, he might have meant Brother Thomas. Certainly Brother Thomas is a holy man. He surely could not have meant Brother Eldred! Eldred is always so crotchety. Though, come to think of it, Eldred is virtually always right. Often, very right. Maybe the rabbi did mean Brother Eldred. But certainly not Brother Phillip. Phillip is so passive, a real nobody. But then, almost mysteriously, he has a gift for somehow always being there for you when you need him. Maybe Phillip is the Messiah. Of course the rabbi didn't mean me, each of them thought in turn about themselves. He couldn't possibly have meant me. I'm just an ordinary person. Yet, suppose he did? Suppose I am the Messiah? Oh, God, not me, each thought. I couldn't be that much for the others. Could I?

As they each contemplated in this manner, the old monks began to treat each other with extraordinary respect on the off chance that one among them might be the Messiah. And on the off chance that each monk himself might be the Messiah, they began to treat themselves with extraordinary respect.

It so happened that people still occasionally came to visit the monastery, to picnic on its green lawn, to wander along its many paths, even to sit in the old chapel to meditate. As they did so, without even being conscious of it, they sensed this aura of extraordinary respect that now began to surround the five old monks and seemed to radiate out from them and permeate the atmosphere of the place.

Hardly knowing why, they began to come back to the monastery more frequently to picnic, to play, to pray. They began to bring their friends to show them this special place. And their friends brought their friends. Then it happened that some of the younger visitors started to talk more and more with the old monks.

After a while, one asked if he could join them. Then another. And another. Within a few years, the monastery had once again become a thriving order and, thanks to the rabbi's gift, a vibrant community of spirituality and light.

As the previous story illustrates, if you consider the combined strength of all your co-workers, it is easy to imagine that a hospital or clinic has the potential to become an inspired center for healing.

A Sense of Community

As described in Buddhism, we surround ourselves with community in order to grow. The intention of the sangha is to support the stabilization of a group's consciousness, so that others even outside the group can feel a soul resonance and be brought into this connection. When we create this type of group synergy, we end up connected with a different sense of belonging.

This, in turn, develops a radiance and vitality that can be quite inspiring to others. Group members become much more deeply engaged at work. In a sense, even our near enemy becomes a part of our support group, as well as others who create emotional upheaval in our workplace. They become fodder for discussion and, in a sense, everyone becomes part of this group, knowingly or not. This can help us wake up from contracted self-preoccupation as we are drawn to expand into something larger than our individual stories. Through our thoughts, words, and actions, we can provide a focal point for further inspiring those around us. Sartre said, "Hell is other people." But it is also true that heaven can be other people. We get to choose.

Choosing to shift our perspective with our co-workers will require many adjustments in our way of thinking. It will require us to use some of the spiritual suggestions from the wisdom traditions. It will require us to learn to interact in, and as, a collective in a different way. In this metamorphosis, gradually old patterns are swept away and a new awareness enters and, by our example, we encourage others to enter into this dialogue with us. This newfound intimacy in our workplace can propel our souls forward, retrieving them from the numbness of our former routines.

Part III: Prognosis

Chapter 8
Toward an Awakened Workplace

"Every result you get in your life is the combination of the challenges you receive from the reality around you and your capacity to respond to that challenge."
—Fred Kofman

We have talked about many forms of relationships—your relationship with yourself, your patients, and your co-workers. As you gradually start to integrate some of the ideas in this book into your professional life, you will begin to understand your behavioral patterns and how they are manifesting themselves in your relationships. In this chapter, we will try to take on what, for most of us, is the most difficult relationship of all—the healthcare system.

We went into healthcare hoping for the nurturance and stability, only to end up finding an emotionally anesthetizing relationship. That relationship often evolves similarly to the one we have with our parents—initially we want them to be everything, we then find out they are not and hold that against them, until finally (it is hoped) we accept that they are human just like us. As with our parents, we often move through a period (though some get stuck there) where we are unable to see the profession's gifts through its wounds. But whenever we see wounds as flaws, we are not accessing the compassion needed to help heal. And, unlike the simpler system of parent and child, medicine is complex with influences coming from within and outside the system.

This chapter focuses on how to direct and apply the principles we have been discussing toward healing the system of healthcare itself.

Dinner Story

In a monastic retreat center in the hills outside of Cinitas, Italy, a couple of monks were just full of loving hospitality. Every week, they would prepare some type of feast and invite a large group of interesting townsfolk to their center. Rich and probing conversations would ensue, and everyone who visited was somehow changed, including the monks and the center.

As time went on, the retreat center had some problems, and the extravagant hospitality once shared had to be directed inward in a time of increasing confusion. Energy just wasn't available for entertaining and hospitality. Many months went by, and there were no more gatherings.

Initially, the usual guests didn't notice this change. But after a prolonged pause, each started feeling a loss. Something was missing, but they couldn't articulate exactly what it was. Gradually, as they saw each other in the village, it started to surface—almost a kind of sadness or regret that the old crowd just wasn't around, and the vitality of the monastery seemed to have dried up. All agreed it was a shame that the monks didn't invite them any more.

One day, a couple of the townsfolk bumped into each other at the bakery and again began lamenting the loss of the gatherings, wondering why the monks had stopped the tradition. "Hey," said the baker, "the monks shouldn't be held responsible for your getting together. You should be."

"He's totally right. Maybe we should create a feast in honor of the monks," suggested one townsperson.

"Yes, a moveable feast, sequentially using each home in our community, as a way to bring back the spirit of our gathering. We can return to the monks that loving hospitality they have showered on us for so many years."

So they set out to invent a new gathering. When assembled, there was the original group with the two monks, but also many new townspeople, a new location and a different intention—the intention of nurturing the monks who had nurtured the town for so long.

Throughout the evening, everyone realized what had been so missed—

the wonderful conversations amid loving hospitality. At the close of the dinner, one of the monks got up to speak.

"So often these types of intentional gatherings are the responsibility of monks and churches. In our previous giving, we felt we had given something away, perhaps given away too much. Somehow we lost our balance. This evening has helped us recognize that giving and receiving are a relationship of balance. Thank you for reminding us of that."

A Crisis of Imbalance

Similar to the monastery, healthcare is in a crisis of imbalance. What has been expected of it and taken from it has not allowed balance. The system seems disconnected from its soul, and spiritual development seems to be absent entirely. Just as individual healthcare workers have had to realize the reciprocal nature and power of their relationships, the collective members of healthcare must realize that reciprocity is necessary for the industry itself to heal.

Medicine is in crises due to its own illness; its own lack of balance. If we do not manifest our collective healing, our wholeness, then just like an out-of-balance patient who cannot mount an appropriate immune response to unhealthy invaders, we too will continue to be susceptible to unwelcome external influences. As discussed in chapter 2, it is rather surprising that instituting a more reasonable work schedule for residents and nurses took the outside influence of lawyers and politicians. How could we, a group of healers with hearts built of compassion, have allowed this type of boot camp training for so many decades?

As happened at the monastery, outsiders had to come in to help us. The legal system helped us to proctor ourselves in a way we had never learned to do for ourselves. Business interests had to come in to help us deal with the lack of balance in the continually escalating costs of healthcare. In so many ways, we have now changed our collective values to reflect the economic logic of the business world, making healthcare into a for-profit endeavor. Maybe healthcare is a place where society should not look to make a profit; maybe it should not be under the same economic logic as the rest of our culture.

We have failed to create an environment of unwavering integrity that might be expected of our field. For many decades, in nearly every poll of esteemed professions, doctors and nurses rated the highest. But we have definitely lost that position in the past fifteen years. How can people look to us to heal them and our society when we cannot even deal with, or heal our own internal issues?

High Tech vs. Human Touch

Sally is a well-trained NICU nurse with many gifts. Often, when a patient is dying or a family is having trouble, the charge nurse will request Sally be assigned to the patient. Sally goes above and beyond, staying often after her shift ends to ensure a smooth transition to the next caretaker. She frequently calls patients and stays connected after a baby dies, and sends annual birthday condolences to the families. Unfortunately, though she has great skills, she doesn't get the same shift differential given to a nurse who specializes in advanced technology, such as ECMO. The system and, over time, her co-workers, fail to value her capabilities justly when compared to the more technologically focused nurses. The nurses with the high-tech training are paid more and held in higher regard.

Notice that most of your continuing education and skill-assessment requirements are focused entirely on mastering tasks and technologies. Judging by the time allotted to these, we seem to value them over the mastery of compassionate presence. This can create feelings of spiritual confusion. Feeling validated for the skills of caring and compassion adds a sense of quality to our lives, something that Sally seems to have been denied. Living in the comparative reality of financial remuneration, we end up feeling that the core values and gifts we have to offer are minimized and even dismissed. Often the problem is not just the people but the way organizations encourage people to think and act—similar to the way a child's social development is judged by his or her grades when it should be judged on broader criteria. This can diminish our collective potential by dismissing some of the crucial qualities that are necessary to be supported and nurtured in an individual caregiver.

Healthcare as Patient

As mentioned in previous chapters, an individual can activate an awakening process to their deepest gifts. It is the same with an organization. How can we apply the same sense of spirituality we have discussed so far to a system? How can we begin to see law, business, and the other influences we seem to resent as our collective near enemy? How can we see these influences as teachers, showing up not to irritate us, but to reveal our wounds, the areas that need healing and expansion?

To begin, we will have to see medicine through the new lens we have developed for ourselves. We have to see it too as an unhealed healer, worthy of our caring and compassion. Instead of blaming the system or making it the architect of our victimization, we will need to bring a very different energy to our encounters with the system. The healthcare system is a patient worthy of healing, worthy of our contemplation. We will need to challenge ourselves to use the resources of our caregiving nature and to direct those energies toward healthcare in much the same way as has been suggested in previous chapters we treat our patients and co-workers. We need to view the system with the same compassion we have for an ailing patient.

It is all too easy in our youth to approach parents and systems with a "What have you done for me lately?" attitude—expecting them to care for us. This is similar to asking the post-op, recovery room patient to take our vital signs. Consider a slight variation of the famous John F. Kennedy quotation and, "Ask not what medicine can do for you, but what you can do for medicine." We have to focus on healing the soul of healthcare. This healing is not about new management, technology, finance, or politics but about the emotional component that is central to healthcare. To revive medicine from its collective burnout, we must ground the system back in its foundation, just as we did for ourselves.

The nucleus of medicine's aim must be healing, and the term "healing" needs to be used in the broadest sense. Healing, on one level, is about maximizing our potential to care for the suffering and needs of others. However, healing is also about how we clean up our internal pollutants and bring a more integrated and conscious self to our profession and system. Healing healthcare is about removing our collective feelings of victimization at the hands of the legal or business systems, so we can move past the stagnation that victimhood fosters.

To confront our wounds and limitations and to heal medicine, we will have to look inward to an individual's personal responsibility for change and to our profession's collective responsibility for changing itself. This empowered, collective awareness will be what eventually changes any system. Focusing on healing in this way will lift us, and medicine, up to new levels of unexplored potential.

The Soul of the System
When we find ourselves listening to and caring for the people around us, our environment changes. Not only do our co-workers and our patients notice the change, but we will also find that coming to work feels different. The hospital or clinic where we previously found so much strife and conflict can now be a place where we feel confident in our ability to effect change. If everyone who walked through the doors of the hospital or clinic could feel healed by the experience, our workplace could become an urban Zen center, a monastic retreat, or a sanctuary of healing. This could be as true for the people who

work in our profession as for the people who come to us to be worked up or worked on.

This change in focus will begin the healing of our system. Although it goes largely unspoken in the modern healthcare paradigm, something invisible within us is either touched and developed, or neglected when we come to work. What can be touched is our compassion; this is where medicine and spirituality come together.

Developing compassion for ourselves and our patients may be a lot easier than developing compassion for the system. There seems to be a large gap between the desires of most healthcare practitioners and the current realities of medicine. This gap between the real and our ideal keeps us longing, when the gap should keep us developing compassion for our dreams and for their eventual integration into the system. By this variation in focus, from longing for what is not to accepting what is, we can access compassion and begin where we truly need to begin—with a transformation of consciousness in healthcare.

A famous quote from Jesus points the way. "I have overcome the world."

Unless he was poorly translated, Jesus did not say "fix" the world. How do we remain in medicine and yet overcome medicine? Can we begin our developmental trajectory and cultivate a refreshed context for healing in this new millennium? First, we will have to stop our complaining and realize something more creative is required of us. This collective healing will largely be determined by what we feel is the purpose or soul of the system. It may be a stretch for some, but maybe the purpose of medicine is similar to the purpose of spirituality—healing into our wholeness.

Remember

It is incredibly tempting to project our conflicts in the workplace on the healthcare system instead of retaining the awareness we developed in previous chapters. When we linger on the problems, we wind up stuck with our potential energy externalized and not enough energy left within for personal, much less collective, change. We end up with a constricted sense of what needs to be done, rarely seeing the eagle's view. As a result, we play small, worrying about our own department or discipline instead of looking at the larger picture of our institution, much less the healthcare system itself.

We have an underlying expectation that the system can care for itself and should also care for us. We must confront an idealized vision of healthcare versus the reality. We should see medicine as a realm where we have to commit our deepest gifts, as opposed to a place where we only look for our expectations to be met.

It can take years to get to the point where you realize what the Jewish tradition says is the highest form of evolution—when the son teaches the father. It may be a slow progression to reach the point where we as healthcare workers can teach the system a new way of being.

The Cycle of Awareness

Steven found himself repeatedly involved in long staff meetings that ended up quite unproductive. His supervisor would bring up a complaint or concern only to find that the rest of the meeting become a session where person after person shared a situation in which something similar affected him or her. After a time, Steve began to wonder if the attendees actually enjoyed the problems because they seemed to be getting some sort of an energy fix from all the meetings instead of trying to implement solutions.

One day he decided to take a chance when his supervisor again brought up several complaints. Steven said, "We spend so much time giving examples of problems, but never focus on the problem enough to get to solution thinking. It is similar to someone complaining about headaches for a decade, even taking Tylenol, but never searching more deeply for the cause. We are beginning to sound like psych patients, talking about the same problems over and over again. I'm not interested in wasting my time in this way. Aren't there some other options here?"

When no amount of reflection enables a group to see what they have not seen before, it is time to expand its collective awareness. Even if there are a plethora of solutions available, we need to get out of the way enough to access them. This consciousness is seldom on the radar screen of most healthcare workers.

We need to create our own reality in the workplace. None of the changes we are talking about involve changing wall colors or food in the cafeteria or even the whole quagmire of office politics. The work described in this book aims at forging a character that is stronger than the environment. This brings us back to the core issue of spirituality as well as issues of meaning and the centrality of purpose.

Seven Ways Individuals Can Help Awaken the Workplace

1. Witnessing

One Buddhist principle, offered earlier in the book, suggests we get to the place where we can stand outside, or *witness* something, to gain a different perspective. This allows for a detachment from our usual dynamics. As in Steven's case above, we can begin to see things differently.

Here is one small suggestion. Step back from the next workplace meeting and do not say a word. Write down every thought you have and, when you feel like sharing, just write over and over: listen, listen, listen. This gives you a wonderful opportunity to observe the energy around what is being shared. It is interesting to notice how frequently something we felt really needed to be said, something we feel that only we could add to the conversation, is added by someone else when we just wait. The things we may have thought were essential to contribute are often more obvious to others than our ego allows us to think.

This exercise can teach us to find a place where we are not sharing what is obvious to everyone, teach us how to get past our need to inject ourselves into each conversation and, instead, seek the reflective contributions that come from observation and stillness. It is a great achievement when a witness can create a place of stillness from which to listen.

If we take a second to consider it, our patients have been asking for a change in our system for some time. Are we listening? We clearly see public demand for change in the hospice movement and in the birthing centers that are being developed. People are making very conscious decisions about where they want to spend their dying days, as well as formulating birthing plans in an attempt to control the consciousness around birth. The public is removing death and birth from hospitals perhaps because they feel as though the consciousness they want around those miraculous transitions is not available to them in hospital environments.

A Nurturing Environment

Robert's mother was dying and she was a very proud woman. She did not want to die in a hospital. She had always thought of hospitals as smelly, sterile, cold and lonely. She requested Robert to have her transferred to the local hospice, so that she could die in a peaceful, warm, loving, and well-attended environment. She did not want to die in the hustle and bustle of a stark, isolating hospital, wearing one of those ugly hospital gowns in a place with such spiritual emptiness.

She also deeply feared that her end-of-life care would be less influenced by her wishes than by the philosophy of her care givers.

A New Consciousness

Sylvia is a new doula (a trained birthing coach) on staff at an academic medical center. She was overheard saying to a family, "If you have to write out a birth plan, you're probably delivering at the wrong place or with the wrong person. A birth plan is giving you a wrong sense of responsibility, making you feel responsible, and often deeply disappointed, when the plan doesn't manifest as you had hoped. But more often than not, your birth will be most influenced by the experience and philosophy of your institution or doctor than by any plan you lay out. Have you ever tried to direct a doctor?" she asked politely. "It's similar to going to a ski lodge and trying to buy a surfboard. They will probably look at you in a strange way.

"Infant massage and massage of pregnant mothers has its place, but to give the obstetrician a massage might even be a better idea—help him or her slow down to the pace of a normal delivery."

Once she relayed to the residents, "What if instead of us giving the baby an Apgar score, the baby gave one to us? What would our heart rate be? What would be our reflex irritability? What would be the tone of our team? But more importantly, are we even aware of our influence on a delivery?"

So instead of trying to find a surfboard at a ski lodge, patients are now trying to find communities of support in places like birthing centers that share their same philosophy. With nearly one-third of hospital deliveries ending up as C-sections, no wonder intelligent people question our hospital system. The assembly-line mentality in today's obstetrical units does not support the quality of consciousness that contemporary mothers seek.

A Collective Spiritual Experience

To make birth and death a spiritual experience, we first have to understand that healthcare is a spiritual experience for everyone involved. Hospice and birthing centers are two great examples of the creativity that can come from an outside-witnessing perspective. Often, like the old-time residency hours, those in the system cannot see from their role-based perspective what is missing. Patients have gone so far as to hire doulas in order to make sure that when the pregnant mother is in her most vulnerable, fearful place, someone is there holding the space in consciousness that the mother wants. Doulas are not always appreciated by the OB nurses. You can imagine the jealousy as the OB nurse ends up charting frantically, thinking all the time that the doula is doing the job the nurse thought she was signing up to do.

The increasing patient interest in alternative medicine suggests that patients feel a loss of connection with the standard healthcare worker. Many healthcare professionals already possess within themselves the spiritual nurturing healer that patients seek, but just cannot find it when nurturing is hidden by their roles. When we discard our nurturing role, we lose enormous healing potential by reducing our thinking to statistics-based treatments that inevitably create feelings of depersonalization on the part of our patients.

Just as an individual can dismiss his or her physical or emotional needs, medicine has dismissed essential parts of itself as well, creating a blatant imbalance of science over spirituality. Sometimes it feels as if the extreme value placed on scientific thinking to the exclusion of other approaches is like a rapidly metastasizing cancer. On and on the denial goes, like cancer therapy undertaken regardless of the physical, emotional, and financial costs, to the patient.

Rule Reversal

Sometimes, we are forced to witness medicine from a different perspective. Our role blurs when we have a relative in the hospital or become a patient ourselves. When a healthcare provider becomes a healthcare consumer, life tends to mature his or her role-based perspective rather quickly. This is a privileged perspective that allows us to witness our profession from a completely different perspective.

Often, we observe that the problem does not lie in the well-intended people or in the system, but in the roles being played.

New Eyes

Tony was suddenly hospitalized. He had worked in the hospital setting for most of his life and knew all the problems. Waking up in the Critical Care Unit (CCU), he came to see that despite the occasional burned-out ward clerk with the quick, unhelpful retorts to his requests, all of the nurses, doctors, and ancillary staff were caring and supportive. Many of them hugged him when they rounded or changed shifts. Nearly all came in and introduced the person taking over the shift. The nutritionist spent more time than imaginable going over his new dietary restrictions.

When he felt down, a resident on call at night came in to tell him,

"It may not be all that helpful to know, but most people having a heart attack go through a sullen phase as they begin to integrate the event into their lives." Tony responded, "Unhelpful? It's totally helpful for you to let me know what is normal. I appreciate you giving me a perspective for this experience. It is so new and such a shock for me."

Tony could see how helpful the extra time, kindness, and explanations were for him. He vowed to try to take a different quality of presence with the people in his care back to his workplace.

Adopting the posture of a witness can transform us. It helps us detach from the usual dynamics of a situation and gives us time to observe things differently. For Tony, this new awareness was the gift from his negative situation. He could now clearly experience what is and is not helpful for a patient. He had a chance to observe in his care providers what fulfilled patients and what drained them. He took home a clearer understanding of the little things that make healing, both for the patient and for the caregiver, more available. Accessing the skill of witness for ourselves can also be richly rewarding to our patients. Tony accessed a metaview of the healthcare system by life placing him in a different role.

As witnesses, we will have a new ability to help patients reframe their suffering or to help them to create a different meaning out of the collapsed story they have about their situation. We cannot share this skill with others if we have not developed it in ourselves.

2. Seek Spiritual Paychecks

Alice's Grand Idea

Alice was concerned with the tension and toxicity she often experienced at the times of shift change. She felt that some of the nurses were time bombs waiting to go off. Some were looking for things that were wrong from the past shift, some were late, and those waiting had to deal with the dismissal and disrespect that form of rudeness entails. Some of the nurses never seemed to be listening to the sign-out, they appeared more interested in getting to their breakfast break.

Alice, convinced this sign-out time wasn't being used wisely, wanted to see if she could develop a different type of interaction to start the work day. So Alice proposed to the administrator something she heard was being done in another hospital in town—something that seemed to stimulate more connection than disconnect. At the beginning of the day, people got together for a quiet time—one of meditation and sharing, not of workplace drama. They started their day with inspirational quotes and focusing on a meditative intention for that day.

She asked the administration to join her in an experiment: Have a group of nurses paid to come in a half-hour early to see if starting the day off differently changed the tone of their unit. The administration promised to consider the trial, but asked Alice if she had read the book, *Punished by Rewards*. She hadn't, so the administrator described a study from the book: Sixteen children were separated into two groups. One group was asked to put together a puzzle and was told that after fifteen minutes, they could stop and have graham crackers. The other group was asked also to spend fifteen minutes putting together a puzzle, and when the time was up they would earn $1 for their efforts. They got graham crackers as well. Interestingly, after the first group finished its crackers, its members all returned to the puzzle to complete it. However, none from the group that got the dollar, returned to the puzzle.

Finally, the administrator told Alice, "I think you have a great idea, but I think what you're trying to achieve should be something your co-workers would be better off doing of their own volition—not something that should have to receive outside validation."

When we look outside for validation or support, we can lose some of the self-reliance we need to develop. It would be nice for Alice to win the administration's support, but would it not be reward enough if the rank and file could change a toxic environment without financial compensation for validation? The paycheck of spiritual development, the paycheck of helping another, and the paycheck of having a fulfilling job can be as rewarding as a monetary paycheck.

Frequently, when we think about remuneration, we do not take into account the spiritual wealth we can accrue at our jobs. Rarely when we discuss our retirement plans do we mention non-material richness, such as the wisdom and understanding we will take into our latter years. How many of us really want the typical businessperson's perspective on retirement—leaving our jobs as early as possible, hoping for years of golfing, and maybe a transition to the best possible retirement home?

Paychecks usually divert our focus to our lives outside the hospital where we have obligations of mortgage, food, and dependents. But once we add a spiritual dimension to our pay, we will begin to appreciate the rewards that go well beyond the economics of our culture. As this spreads through our collective, we will be better able to bring other values to the current bottom-line thinking.

When someone understands that the connections we share are a form of payment, they can consciously decide if some promotion really provides a raise, or if the managerial role being offered actually diminishes their spiritual paycheck. Once you get to this point and connect with others, you may decide that more money and a management position do not offer the spiritual rewards of your current connections with patients. While it is flattering to be offered a job at a higher level, it may not be worth it if that means a diminishment in remuneration on a level of connection or spiritual development.

We need to reevaluate our priorities. Do I want a dream home or do I prefer to have a dream life? How can I have a dream life without a job that is aligned with my deepest personal vision? To have a career that is aligned with our dream is a great achievement; something few will ever know. This is something eminently possible for healthcare workers.

Usually all the buzz about corporate loyalty comes at the expense of our deeper truth. What if loyalty was to arise from a devotion to one's expanding spiritual path? To one's personal healing? A forward-thinking institution would be a place where jobs nurtured the spiritual path and growth, first and foremost. It would be a place that nurtured the soul with an environment suited to creative expression. It is not too much of a stretch to see how this can play out in retention in the workplace. One definition of success is to get to a place in life where we do not have to work with people not on our level.

3. Adopting Another's Perspective

Tithing Our Time

Mary reflected on the fact that her religion asked a tithing of 10 percent and she began thinking about tithing at work—not simply money, but other types of tithing, such as time and ideas. She decided to start volunteering at her workplace, or at least to change her perspective about the time she already volunteered.

Mary had developed a massage protocol for infants and taught parents infant massage. She also had a research study tagged on to her efforts. The study took more time than she dreamed, and she had no support for her efforts, except for her own evolving perspective about infants and massage. She decided to change her perspective from one of resentment for the lack of support, to one where she did this willingly as a volunteer in her free time.

A simple change in perspective changed her reality. After this change, she noticed other nurses coming in to be infant cuddlers in their free time and one nurse became a volunteer doula in the maternity unit.

This sort of community transformation can only happen when we have radically altered our perspective. A healthy sense of altruism can show us how our workplaces can been seen as sacred. This is where practicing personal inquiry affects a larger group and those effects can germinate the seeds of a larger collective inquiry.

Healthcare-professional support groups, as mentioned previously, can be places for spiritual breastfeeding until we are developed enough to walk on our own.

In India, it is felt that nothing of importance can be developed by someone alone, a trilogy of energies is needed. In the trilogy are the combined energies of people who are manifestors, those who are visionaries, and those who attract and circulate the energy of money. These three separate archetypal consciousnesses need to come together to create. In contrast, in Western medical academia, one person has to think up a project, write it up, raise the money, do the research, compile the data, run the statistics, submit, and hopefully get their work published. No wonder creativity is a bit stymied.

4. Find What Inspires You

To cultivate a more creative awareness in our workday, we need to retrieve a spaciousness that allows us to view things differently. We must find the still points in our day when we pause, when we hold a baby, or when we confront the direct honesty of a patient on his or her death bed and allow those times to awaken a tenderness that no task-oriented endeavor can.

Reaching our full potential as healers is of the utmost importance when we talk about the expanded perspectives of healing. We must have the space and time to reflect and be in touch with our interior life.

Nurturing Tenderness

Members of a wisdom circle were given the task to come up with things in their day that they do, or have done, to nurture their tenderness. The list was as long as it was delightful. Many mentioned physical foci in their day that they use as a touch point or altar for their consciousness.

One nurse said that when she entered her locked unit, a four-digit code needed to be punched in. She said she remembered the code through kinesthetic memory so that she didn't have to focus on it any longer and, instead, when entering the code, she'd pretend she was spelling out the word "love." She felt that this helped her refocus her energies in a spiritual direction during the numerous times she entered her unit.

A pediatrician said that on his office phone he had a sticker that read, "A man can't know what it's like to be a mother." Each time he picked up the phone, he was reminded of the level of compassion he hoped to embrace.

Another nurse said that she tried to walk very slowly and match her breath to that pace on her way in from the hospital parking lot in the morning. After spending an hour in rush-hour traffic, she wanted to transform her quality of attention to something other than the feelings of road rage.

Other participants mentioned journaling or meditating during their breaks. One nurse said that each time she entered a new space, whether it was opening a door, opening an isolate, or picking up the phone, she'd take a deep breath and recite to herself, "This is an opportunity to be open to a new experience."

Sustaining a meditative awareness at our workplace requires at least some tricks or helpful hints. It is helpful to have various sources of inspiration sprinkled throughout our day as a way to stay in touch with our higher intentions. Find what inspires you and use it for as long as it works. If it eventually loses its energy, find something else that works. Tricks, like the pediatrician's note or taking a deep breath with each new experience, can remind us to communicate with as much compassion and love as possible.

5. Open New Connections

Bob's New Vision

Bob, an OR tech who clashed frequently with an infamously perfectionist ophthalmologist, decided to see if he could instigate a change in their relationship. He realized that he needed to learn to take what the surgeon said seriously, but not personally, though taking things personally was a long-time habit. He needed to learn to disregard the surgeon's attitude, not inject his sense of self into the discussion.

After the next biting comment, instead of reacting by closing up, Bob said very calmly, "As you know, I'm always looking for ways to improve my work. I want you to know I am grateful for your observations. I'd like to apologize for my part in this situation."

Bob said this even though he didn't really think the situation was, to any degree, his fault. But he'd arrived at the point where he'd rather be happy than right—rather stay connected than be right. Interestingly, once the surgeon felt heard and/or acknowledged, their relationship changed dramatically.

The mere opening of a connection with an apologetic tone brings openness and can change the stance of the other person. Often people will shift before your eyes. However, first we have to learn to listen for the energy behind a problem or complaint and not just to the complaint itself. Listening this way can reveal soul pains in our patients, our co-workers, and in the system at large. Sometimes, all one needs is for us to be a witness to their pain, distress, or confusion. Our state of consciousness or presence can reflect back to them a different option in tone or understanding.

Having people with these skills allows a collective to gradually shift from the hierarchical structures we have been trained to see to a more holographic understanding; what the new age philosopher Ken Wilber calls a holoarchy. This is the beginning of coming together in a new way of engagement with those we work with—a way that is based more on their spiritual achievements than on meritocracy or the initials after a name.

6. Minimize Hierarchy

Hierarchies can keep us divorced from our highest potential because personal integrity can become entirely secondary to a role-based, ask-no-questions tone. In a hierarchy, workers generally have to agree with their superior. But as seen with many spiritual teachers, it is often the enlightened loner, the person neither in the hierarchy nor in the system, who can sow a seed of more equanimity in relatedness.

Housekeeping Insights

On morning rounds, when a patient is going through a troubled time, Dr. Sam will seek out Norma, a hospital housekeeper. Through the years, he's learned of her ability to connect with patients, lend a listening ear, and share some remarkable spiritual wisdom. He once listened in on a conversation she had with a patient after Dr. Sam requested that she "tidy up the patient's room." This became their code for her to lend her listening ear.

He noticed that she never asked questions about the patients' diseases, rather she asked about their life before the disease, the interruption the disease had caused, and their plans for the future. He marveled at her skill, wishing he could muster her same availability.

We need to realize that our hierarchical systems are part of the problem stunting our potential. Anyone who has served on an ethics committee knows the multidisciplinary makeup of the committee brings richness to the discussions. We have a lot of rich potential in our midst, both inside our profession and in the connections we develop with other fields. Sometimes it takes an outsider for us to see that potential, as the following story, a mass internet junk mailing, reveals.

The Carpenter

Once upon a time, two brothers who lived on adjoining farms fell into conflict. It was the first serious rift in forty years of farming side by side, sharing machinery, and trading labor and goods as needed. Then the long collaboration fell apart. It began with a small misunderstanding and grew into a major difference, finally exploding into an exchange of bitter words followed by weeks of silence.

One morning there was a knock on the door of John, the older brother. He opened it to find a man with a carpenter's toolbox.

"I'm looking for a few days of work," he said. "Perhaps you have a few small jobs here and there. Could I help you?"

"Yes," said John. "I do have a job for you. Look across the creek at that farm. That's my neighbor. In fact, it's my younger brother. Last week there was a meadow between us. He took his bulldozer to the river levee and now there is a creek between us. Well, he may have done this to spite me, but I'll go him one better. See that pile of lumber curing by the barn? I want you to build me a fence—an eight-foot-high fence—so I won't need to see his place anymore. That'll cool him down, anyhow."

The carpenter said, "I think I understand the situation. Show me the nails and the post-hole digger and I'll be able to do a job that pleases you."

John had to go to town for supplies, so he helped the carpenter get the materials ready and then he was off for the day.

The carpenter worked hard all that day, measuring, sawing, nailing. About sunset, when the farmer returned, the carpenter had just finished his job. The farmer's eyes opened wide and his jaw dropped. There was no fence there at all. It was a bridge—a bridge stretching from one side of the creek to the other! A fine piece of work, handrails and all, and the neighbor, his younger brother, were coming across with his hand outstretched.

"You are quite a fellow to build this bridge after all I've said and done."

The two brothers met in the middle, taking each other's hand. They turned to see the carpenter hoist his toolbox on his shoulder.

"No, wait! Stay a few days. I've a lot of other projects for you," said John.

"I'd love to stay on," the carpenter said, "but, I have many more bridges to build."

7. Inviting Spirituality Back

One often helpful outsider who we have largely and regrettably lost is the hospital chaplain.

A Minister's Story

For many years, Reverend Summers served as the only chaplain in a large hospital. But, he never felt truly comfortable in the hospital because he didn't have a medical background and seldom received counsel from the medical team. He felt out of place because the hospital staff was so technologically oriented that his message of comfort was overlooked by the other people involved in the healing process. Rev. Summers believed that ministry and healthcare were related because both focused on the deeper meaning of life. But instead of feeling welcome to share his expertise with healthcare workers and learn from theirs, he felt dismissed.

The diminished presence of faith-based ministers from our hospitals is a true casualty of modern healthcare. With the gradual dismissal of the importance of this perspective, we have lost a lot of healing potential for both the patients and the workers. What used to be an environment in which spiritual comfort and support had an important place has now become a technology-based place in which spiritual care and prayer does not seem to fit beyond brief visits.

The Evolution of Healing

Maybe once we pull back the curtain on the influences of business and law we will find, like Dorothy in *The Wizard of Oz*, not some all-powerful wizard but simply a well-intended role being played on the parts of these other fields. A role we can help them expand by expanding our own. Individuals who awaken from a role to their fuller potential tend to be society's bridge builders or connectors.

We can be society's healers once we have healed ourselves as a collective. Then healthcare can have an influence on other systems by helping them to connect in new, creative, and healthier ways.

To usher in a new collective alignment around the deepest truth of our profession will take some creative emergence by us all. When this occurs, we will be proud participants in the evolution of healing instead of the apologetics we often feel for our field at this time.

Our profession has a different nature with unique gifts to offer our society. Business operations were not at the top of our priority list since most of us went into the healing arts due to an undeniable soul tug to help others. Most of us never considered rationing that assistance. We have to be aware that this perspective is a gift. It is a gift to our society. Until we embrace that gift, the larger potential of our profession to influence and heal the systems with which we interact will be minimal.

Institutions evolve as the consciousness in them evolves. Medicine will evolve as healers evolve. What awaits us is a chance to more fully become who we really are and all that we have the potential to be, both individually and collectively.

We cannot change the current model by fighting and complaining, we need a change in consciousness, a new way of thinking that makes the existing model obsolete. Using the principles in this text, a new creativity will become available for our expansion. The wisdom of our psychological and our spiritual traditions has the ability to transform our workplace stagnation. We need these ideas and guides to direct us toward alternate ways to view science, medicine, and caring, especially as they relate to the evolution of humanity as a whole.

Gena's Changing Perspective

Gena had three children all less than three years of age. Suddenly, she was diagnosed with a metastatic lymphoma. After months of treatment, her cancer went into remission. She relayed, "My cancer went into remission and I'm still here. But the Gena who is here—the mother, the wife that you see today—is not the same Gena who was diagnosed with lymphoma a year ago. I've certainly developed a more mature consciousness."

She began to talk about the deeper layers of the experience of her cure, as well as her healing into a different understanding of meaning in her life. Her illness and recovery initiated inquiry, self-discovery, and a change in her perspective of daily life. She began to have gratitude for the gifts that are so apparent once she was compelled to take a different point of view on life.

The problems in healthcare will not change until the above layers of experience are integrated enough that we begin to change our thinking and look for new and creative ways to develop.

Chapter 9
A Continually Deepening Experience

"More than any skill or product, the way in which we align our work with our deepest life intuitions will be the genuine contribution we make to the emerging world community."
—*Rick Jarow*

The healthcare system is deadening the creative spirit and the spiritual life of many of its physicians, nurses, and other caregivers. To reconnect healing with creativity and spirituality, this book has looked at the psychological and spiritual aspects of a healthcare provider's personal interactions at work. Changing the matrix of healthcare means creating a more profound personal connection between spirituality and healing—something big enough and deep enough to sustain the humanity of healthcare workers. We must then take that spirituality and apply it to our patients, our co-workers, and the healthcare system itself.

The suggestions offered in this book are meant to help the sensitive healer in us bloom. The garden of healthcare has many weeds. We can continue to blame others for this overgrowth, or we can take responsibility for not being attentive gardeners and begin the work of uprooting and replanting.

Much of medicine's spiritual wisdom seems to have been lost. To harvest and retrieve this lost dimension in our workplace requires centering our work on principles that do not change. We must let the wisdom of the contemplative traditions touch, change, and heal medicine. In this way, we can retrieve the healing arts as a metaphor for the mystical experience, a continuing search for personal and collective deepening.

A Roadmap Out

We have attempted to illustrate the contribution spirituality can bring to our workplace. We even suggest that it offers a roadmap out of our current stagnation. The hypnotism of our social conditioning can be broken by seeking the path of personal and spiritual deepening. It is essential for us to try on a new model based on a spiritually inspired vision that stabilizes a higher consciousness. This higher consciousness will then allow us to access an expansion in our vocation.

Our current medical model is a mirror of how we participate in other systems, such as our family and our society. As a nation, for instance, we base our success largely on our economic stability, and many businesses (and hospitals) do the same. But while healthcare may have the same problems as these other systems, it also has the same opportunity to look at its future with fresh eyes.

The technological aptitude we have developed may be well-honed, but we have misplaced something in our educational system as well as in our career trajectories. Renewing the spiritual part of our nature is essential to support our continual growth. In fact, this is crucial in order to discover a deeper dimension of ourselves, other people, and the evolutionary potential of our field. When we rediscover the belief held among all major indigenous traditions, we realize we are healers who work on holy ground. Caring and giving have been closely associated with spirituality for as long as recorded history. We hope to have reminded you of this lost dimension.

We have the power to reown the identity that is rightfully ours. The question is, can we evolve a more systematic way of integrating spiritual principles in our workday?

By reinfusing spirituality back into healthcare, we can then begin working from the deepest truth of our field. Bringing this truth into focus leads us away from medicine as strictly a scientific endeavor toward a more expanded context. From here, we can tap into the deepest energies of our creative potential. Finding this creative potential will require awareness, presence, diligent discovery, and the integration of the psychological and spiritual principles found in this book.

Here's an example:

Kyle's Expansion

Dr. Kyle has been on his hospital ethics committee for years and enjoys the continual education required of its members. The multidisciplinary framework of the committee gave him a chance to view the opinions and skills of the other professionals in his hospital. He could clearly see the richness brought to cases by these various points of view.

Often during consult discussions, when other physicians would voice strong opinions, he'd hold back, explaining that in this arena a doctor's view carried no more weight than the housekeeper. The sense of entitlement he once felt as a physician had gradually melted as he started to see the rich perspectives of others. He appreciated developing the ability to stay open to all viewpoints before making his own decision.

Kyle knew his hospital was embarking on the construction of a new building that would translate into a huge debt for years. He was excited about discussing the pressures this would add to their system, how it might change nursing ratios, environmental issues, and the like. He wondered if they could bring into the equation the larger social and spiritual aspects that need to be integrated into modern healthcare as well as into our culture. What gifts could this shift bring?

He knew from his own life how hard it was to move from financial motivation to higher aspirations. He knew it had taken him years of personal work and contemplation to see the social and spiritual paychecks in his work.

Dr. Kyle had discovered the inherent richness in his work and in the potential of medicine. Like Dr. Kyle, if we do the personal work and contemplation, we will also find the deeper meaning in our jobs. We can allow our jobs to become deep expressions of our spiritual natures. By reinfusing spirituality as a principle, we can invite a creative emergence into our stagnant system.

In the Buddhist tradition, it is said that knowledge without wisdom does not mean much. We see this in patients who search the Internet for information about their condition; coming up with all sorts of unusual therapies and a bottomless pit of confusing information. They get information, but lack the wisdom of discernment and lack the ability to integrate the new knowledge into their situation. Like our patients, when we have the scientific knowledge without wisdom, we end up with superficial encounters with our patients and with ourselves.

A Creative Revolution
If we follow the path laid out in this book, we can begin a creative revolution in healthcare. As new qualities emerge in us, an expanded definition of healing and of our workplace encounters will also surface. Slowly, medicine will transform as we do. It may seem daunting to consider ourselves as key players in changing an enormous system, but many larger cultures have been

softened by a small pocket of authentically spiritual people. It takes time, but these small pockets of people slowly, carefully, responsibly, and humbly begin to grow an influence. The work of encouraging a collective expansion in our vocation is an essential part of our ongoing professional development.

Dr. Kyle again illustrates this process:

Dr. Kyle listened to a lecture from Cynda Rushton, a nurse-ethicist from Johns Hopkins, who described the concept of organizational ethics. To him, the lecture brilliantly extended all he'd learned on the hospital ethics committee. This model of collective inquiry balanced various inputs to get the highest and fairest thinking available.

Having seen the richness of this collective inquiry applied to bedside ethics, he began to see its applicability in addressing other issues at the hospital. He wanted to take this same model of inquiry to the corporate decision makers.

Many at his hospital complained that the administration would benefit from a larger vision than that provided by the financial wizards on the board of directors. Kyle thought the model that worked so well with patient ethics might be used as a template for dialogue on a corporate level, allowing fair weight to all the various voices in the system, as well as balancing the competing priorities. He felt this might be a great way to put spirituality and compassion side-by-side with the realities of finance instead of having them lurk beneath the ever present financial priorities. This thinking led him to propose a new construct for the business organization of hospital.

In the next meeting, Kyle began the discussion with an abstract question instead of focusing directly on some hot topic. He asked the group, "What do you think are the underlying causes of our overspending in healthcare?"

He was delighted at how quickly the group began discussing the often unrealistic expectations our society has for healthcare. He thought if someone could eliminate or temper some of these unreasonable expectations, especially the extreme measures taken around death, a degree of financial freedom might come back to the system.

One committee member recalled a statistic from a political speech that claimed that more than a third of healthcare dollars are spent in the last five days of someone's life. Kyle was pleased that the discussion got past the usual focus on the macroenvironment of a hospital. If we could see death with a more spiritual perspective, he thought, we could perhaps see it as a miracle similar to birth. And if we could transform the way we die, we'd probably end up transforming the way we live as well.

By changing the collective way we view death, by embracing other perspectives than our typical, material-based consciousness, we could expand to a more consciousness-based paradigm and the money pit of healthcare in our society might be alleviated. Changing our expectations, Kyle felt, could change the monetary realities.

Like Dr. Kyle and his group, we have the opportunity to focus on the deeper causes of our complaints; the deeper meanings of our stagnation. But we must be able to think it before we can translate that deeper meaning into action. Changing your perspective inevitably leads to changing the way you interact.

Social Artistry
Those who take the time to learn the lessons of burnout, delve into their psychological and spiritual deepening, and learn how to apply that to their relationships become not only happier, but represent the human potential movement integrated into healthcare. When this begins to happen, we will have truly activated our deepest calling as healers and begun to embody the role of social artists, pointing society to new ways to view healing.

In this social artistry lies the creativity of the healing arts. We can find our humanity and activate a renewed sense of sacredness to a world that dreadfully needs a new perspective. As Maya Angelou said, "It's time for thinking people to think." It is also time for healing people to heal. If we do, healthcare could become a powerful collective force for healing society as a whole.

Awakening this human potential is neither just for ourselves, nor simply for medicine, it is an opportunity for us to be an example to other professions of the fact that, when people do their own inner work, they can transform their profession into a vehicle for more conscious and sacred actions in the world. Deep down, we all want to work for something beyond our paycheck, our possessions, and even beyond our personal development.

We are the people who wanted to change the world. Now we see that we *can*.

Make a vow today to be apart of this continuing dialogue. Become an active participant in transforming our profession and you will be rewarded with rich understandings of our collective healing and begin to uncover the emerging future of human consciousness.

Each generation outdoes the last. That is the bedrock of evolution. We must give ourselves the permission to outdo those who have come before us and to be outdone by those who follow. Let us begin developing an authentic spirituality that can be integrated into healthcare and become the new cornerstone of a transformed healthcare system. We have the power to create the identity that we love, but we need to do the work to get there. Let us, the pioneers, usher in this new change.

34828515R00080

Made in the USA
San Bernardino, CA
08 June 2016